HALLELUJAH!
The Extraordinary Story of
Shaun Ryder and Happy Mondays

John Warburton
with Shaun Ryder

To Rach,
and all the folks at Ashtray Weekly

This edition first published in 2003 by
Virgin Books Ltd
Thames Wharf Studios
Rainville Road
London
W6 9HA

Reprinted 2004

First Virgin paperback edition published in Great Britain in 2000 by Virgin Publishing Ltd

A catalogue record for this book is available from the British Library.

ISBN: 0 7535 0781 1

Photo section by Random Design
Typeset by TW Typesetting, Plymouth, Devon
Printed and bound in Great Britain by Mackays of Chatham plc

CONTENTS

Thanks to (in no order of preference):

The Mondays, for everything.
Smithy at the *Sport*, for his version of events.
Shed Seven, for giving in to the dark side.
Xena Warrior Princess, for leather.
Chris Moyles, for tongue.
Steve Lamacq, for the chat.
Fatboy Slim, for the insight.
Me Mam and Dad, for me.
Briggy Smale, for looking like a policewoman.
Tony Livesey, and everyone else at the *Daily Sport*, for the good times.
Clint Boon, for the Bez thing.
Phil Saxe, for remembering what everyone else has forgotten.
Anthony H Wilson, for the pint.
Neil Mather, for . . . er, good point?
Carl 'Mad Dog' Royle, for the pictures.
Damien Hirst, for sharks and skulls and stuff.
Keith Allen, for eventually sorting it out.
Nigel Pivaro, for flushing Shaun's head down the bog at school.
Tom Bruggen, for his superhuman tolerance, and ability to talk faster than anyone else on the planet.
SJM, for the record.
Ed and Di, for practical jokes.
Dionysus, for the wine.
The Sci-Fi Channel, for *Lost In Space* and *Lexx*.
G-man, for being there.
Martin Herbert, for . . .
Ian and Mel at Virgin Publishing, for sorting it.
Admiral, for the T-shirt.
Anthony at Gio Goi, for the wardrobe.
Jimmy The Gent, Dom and Rocky, for their regular charity work, especially with starving Albanians.
Jo Whiley, for being an Amazonian sex goddess.
Gene and Delakota, for putting up with me in nets.
Various publicity people, for . . . fuck all! (you know who you are)
Dave at the Greenhouse, for the stories and the pictures.
Manchester United, for beating Juventus.

If I've missed you, I'm sorry. But thanks anyway. In fact I've left a few gaps below so you can fill your own details in. Thanks for reading, anyway. And if you're looking here before you actually start the book, then the butler did it. Tara!

. . . ., for . . . .
. . . ., for . . . .

DRAMATIS PERSONAE

Shaun Ryder – aka **X**. Former postman from Little Hulton, Salford, turned singer/songwriter for Happy Mondays and Black Grape. Hooligan prophet, ghetto poet. Reformed Happy Mondays 'to pay off the fucking taxman'. Big nose. Obsessed with people's heights.

Mark Berry – aka **Bez**. Friendly, grinning, wide-eyed loon. Walking chemical set. Became a cultural icon by shaking maracas and jigging about. Now lives in a cottage near Glossop, where he occasionally stages indoor motorbike rallies.

Paul Ryder – aka **Horse**. Happy Mondays bassist. Shaun's younger brother and long-time sparring partner. Spent the years since Happy Mondays split in 1993 in and out of rehab. At time of writing, not talking to Shaun.

Gaz Whelan – aka **Ronnie**. Salford-born Happy Mondays drummer. Almost made a career as a professional footballer with Everton. A lucky escape, obviously. Once tried to have sex with a beanbag.

Mark Day – aka **Cowhead, Moose**. Former Mondays guitarist. Swore when he left the band that he'd never work again with Shaun, whom he perceives as 'an animal and a nutcase'. Claims to have never heard of Black Grape. Now sells books door-to-door.

Paul Davis – aka **PD, Knobhead**. Original Happy Mondays keyboard player. Regards Shaun as 'a penis'. Regarded by Shaun, in turn, as 'an idiot' and 'a fucking tosser'.

Paul Wagstaff – aka **Wags**. Guitarist in Manchester band Paris Angels who teamed up with Shaun to play guitar for Black Grape and then replaced Mark Day when the Mondays reformed. Oddly proud of his moustache. His biggest fear is being stabbed to death by clowns.

Nuts – aka **Peanut** or – his real name – **Marlon Vegas**. Met Shaun when the singer went AWOL in Ibiza for three weeks, then joined the reformed Mondays as a singer/dancer/vibes merchant.

Derek Ryder – aka **Horseman**. Shaun and Paul's dad. Always travelled with the original Mondays to 'look after them'. Opposed to band's reunion.

Gary Marsden – aka **G-man**. Long-time pal of Shaun Ryder. Sacked from Mondays entourage after unfortunate chemicals-related accidental robbery incident.

Rowetta – aka **Row**. Mondays' backing singer who also appeared on Simply Red's *Stars* album. Ex-singing teacher. The reason that the Mondays have no groupies.

Tony Wilson – Granada TV newsreader who founded Manchester's legendary Factory Records and signed Joy Division, New Order and the Mondays. Thinks Shaun Ryder is cleverer than Shakespeare and Proust. Genuinely.

Nathan McGough – son of sixties Liverpool poet Roger McGough. Managed Happy Mondays for majority of their career.

Paul Oakenfold – aka **Oakey**. Legendary trail-blazing acid house DJ who remixed early Mondays tracks and produced *Pills 'N' Thrills And Bellyaches*.

Neil Mather – Long-suffering freelance tour manager prone to pranks and practical jokes. Also frequently the victim thereof.

Ben Leach – Scouse keyboardist formerly in The Farm who replaced Paul Davis in reunited Mondays. A sickly child who gets very upset when he loses his coat.

Tom Bruggen – aka **Too-Nice Tom**. World's nicest man. Filmed *The Grape Tapes* documentary. Put up – and put up with – Shaun in his home in Burnley when the singer was detoxing from smack.

Tony Livesey – managing director and editor in chief of the acid bath of British culture which is the *Daily Sport*. Took on Shaun as a celebrity columnist. Regretted it.

Marc Smith – aka **Smithy/Mr Potato Head/Talking Egg**. Non-hirsute sports editor of the *Daily Sport*. Ghost-wrote Shaun's column on the newspaper but came to a sticky end after notorious trip to Ibiza, during which he puked off a balcony after smelling Shaun's reeking feet.

Simon Moran – concert promoter who founded SJM Promotions. The man who persuaded the Mondays to re-form.

Chris Moyles – chubby Radio One DJ and Mondays fan. Normally referred to by Shaun as 'Dave Pearce'.

Clint Boon – bowl-headed keyboardist from Inspiral Carpets, now fronting Clint Boon Experience.

Martin Hannett – Manchester record producer famous for his work with Joy Division and his prodigious drug intake. Produced Mondays' second album, *Bummed*. Died in 1991.

Lee Mullen – Mancunian drum teacher who played percussion on the reunion tour. Big mates, bizarrely, with ex-Man U goalkeeper Peter Schmeichel.

Martin Herbert – aka **King Dong**. Guitar technician. Made front page of *Daily Sport* after incident involving his knob and an unfortunate Brazilian chambermaid named Maria.

Nigel Pivaro – aka **Terry Duckworth** from *Coronation Street*. Went to school with Shaun (on rare days that Shaun went) and now a huge Mondays fan. Once jibbed into a hotel in Paris.

Oriole Leitch – daughter of sixties hippy singer Donovan. Shaun's common-law wife, estranged following the split of Black Grape.

Astrella Leitch – younger daughter of Donovan, ex-common-law wife of Paul Ryder.

Briggy Smale – aka **B**. Spoilsport Radio One employee who, in Ibiza, refused to whap her baps out for £200.

John Warburton – aka **Warbs**. Ex-showbiz editor of *Daily Sport* who ghost-writes Shaun's weekly column, 'It's Great Talking Straight' for the same paper. Once forced to slap out small fire in socks on roof of Mondays' tour bus. Butt of many jokes, subject of many pranks. Author of this mighty book.

INTRODUCTION

The air was electric, sparking, that rare, one-in-a-million occasion when the event might actually prove to be better than the anticipation. This was the moment which thousands had longed to see. They were crammed together to witness a magic spectacle, a history-defining moment. All tickets had sold out just hours after they'd gone on sale, and now they were being dispensed for upwards of £100 each by gleeful touts.

In the changing rooms, a few choice words were exchanged as everyone got ready. This really was do-or-die time. Soon, it would be time to head out and face the crowd. The cheering, the applause and the sheer expectancy weighed on every single soul like a lead life-jacket, forcing them to take deep breaths in their determination to stay cool.

Of course, they all realised, it was the fans who had put them where they were. The fans had paid to see them play, made them famous, and kept their names alive while other, lesser lights were forgotten. The fans had crowned them kings, and they owed their status to them.

Yes, their fans had given them life, and that was why they had to perform. The in-fighting, back-biting and shifty politics of recent times had to be put behind them. For this exercise they were a team, and they would give 100 per cent to the event tonight.

A Scottish accent spoke out in the dressing room between hearty chews on a well-masticated piece of Wrigleys Extra.

'Right, let's fucking do it,' said the boss.

'Let's fucking do it,' answered his boys.

And so they walked out, on to the cavernous stage awaiting them. The crowd responded with mass adulation, frenziedly chanting, singing, whistling and waving flags. The date was 21 April 1999. The venue was the Stadio Delle Alpi in Turin. And the fixture was Manchester United v Juventus in the semi-finals of the 1999 Champions League – an opportunity for United to reach the final of Europe's premier club tournament for the first time since 1968. Not since the days of Best, Law and Charlton had Manchester reached these rarefied heights.

The referee blew his whistle for kick-off. Meanwhile, many thousands of miles away, in a tiny leisure centre in the English Midlands, Mark Berry, Gaz Whelan and Shaun Ryder were shouting at a television screen:

'Come on you fucking Reds!'

Happy Mondays were also facing their own spectacular, large-scale public event tonight. They were sitting backstage at Hereford Leisure Centre preparing for their first live show in six years. The band who had single-handedly invented baggy, Madchester and, allegedly, imported Ecstasy to the north west of England, were poised for an unlikely, monumental comeback ... but, for the moment, bugger that. This was the European semi, and United needed a victory in Turin.

The game was a cracker. Juventus went 2–0 up early doors, and United's dream of European dominance appeared dead. Surely the Mancs couldn't come back from this. Yet amazingly they rallied, and goals from Roy Keane, Dwight Yorke and a late winner from

Andy Cole took them through to the final against Bayern Munich. The scenes of rejoicing in Turin and Manchester were matched only by the excessive celebrations backstage at Hereford.

Then the celebrations were cut short.

'Happy Mondays to the stage,' came the shout over the radios.

This was it.

Hallelujah! The boys were back in town.

1. FUNKY JUNKIES CRACK CHARTS

Mondays play New York lying down, Shaun bites Gaz's head, Bez spits at armed man, Shaun is caught selling Eddy Grant's sofa for crack, the Mondays make Brian Tilsley cry and Shaun doesn't sell his arse for 50p.

On 16 October 1998 the former artist/singer/writer/thief/thug/junkie/actor known as Shaun Ryder said there was no way the Happy Mondays would get back together.

Six weeks later he'd changed his mind.

That's Shaun Ryder in a nutshell. A living, smoking, drinking, joking, singing paradox of epic rock'n'roll proportions, a hypocrite who hates hypocrites.

He's the Salford council estate lad turned superstar who found a dream life and a dream wife, then lost the lot.

Shaun Ryder is the man who can look you in the eye and tell you he's quit heroin while emptying a bag of brown powder on to a piece of tinfoil. He's the man who can have you rolling around the floor in stitches one minute with an impromptu stand-up routine, and then reaching for the razor blade the next. That said, he's also a genius and one of the lads, and when he said he was getting the Happy Mondays back together, I'm glad I was there – and, as the showbiz editor on the *Daily Sport* charged with the task of ghosting Shaun's weekly column, I soon found myself right in the thick of the surreal odyssey of the Mondays' reunion.

Life around Shaun Ryder is never boring. To some he's an enigma, a Salford sphinx weaving riddled, fractured lyrics into unforgettable anthems. To others he's a Morrissey, a Jim Morrison, a Neil Young, a poet/prophet guru from the gutter. To many more, of course, he's simply a dodgy wanker with a big nose.

So why did Shaun Ryder, against all his earlier protestations, decide to re-form Happy Mondays? The answer is caught up in a terrifying tax bill, a messy separation, a bedsit in Burnley and stomach implants undertaken in a bid to kick a bad smack habit (are there any *good* ones?). It's a tale which, along the way, involves a staged orgy which made front-page tabloid news, a skull on a stick given to Bez by Britpop artist Damien Hirst, and a sexual assault on a horse in Dublin (who, by all accounts, enjoyed it).

Nobody who had witnessed the acrimonious and anarchic break-up of the original Happy Mondays could ever have thought that this bunch of gifted chancers and inspired hooligans could ever re-form. The end seemed too bloody, too messy for that. There was too much bad feeling.

But the Mondays have always been a mass of contradictions, a perverse play of contrary tensions and impulses. They've always made absolute sense by making no sense at all. And, to understand the daft inevitability and unique (il)logic of their comeback, it's helpful to consider the manner in which they first got together, right back at the start of the eighties.

You may know some of this story already. But you certainly won't know all of it.

Shaun William Ryder and his brother Paul first formed a 'band' called Happy Mondays in 1980, when the duo were in their late teens, 'for something to do, like'

(Shaun). A succession of Scally mates joined them to muck around on a handful of battered instruments and spliff away long hours in rehearsal studios like the space beneath Manchester's Boardwalk club and in guitarist Mark 'Cowhead' Day's loft.

The early, fledgling Mondays soon settled down to a nucleus of the Ryder brothers – Shaun singing, Paul on bass – Mark Day, drummer Gaz Whelan and keyboardist Paul Davis. Gaz had joined at fifteen, after somehow mistaking Shaun for David Bowie while waiting at a bus stop in Salford. The band had even somehow wangled a deal with legendary Manchester label Factory Records, run by local entrepreneur and newsreader Tony Wilson.

Tellingly, in these early days the Mondays were also becoming known for their sartorial sensibility. They'd started buying flares from a market stall run by Phil Saxe, a former marketing manager for a frozen food company who had connections with Factory. Saxe was to eventually end up managing Happy Mondays after they approached him in the Hacienda. However, he'd already seen the lads coming in to his shop and spotted them for their beatnik looks and penchant for flares, a trend which seemed to be coming alive in a small part of Salford.

PHIL SAXE: The Mondays used to come to my stall to buy 20″ flared cords. They had little goatee beards and big baggy jumpers, sort of beatniks, and were completely different from the sort of people you were used to seeing. Then I met them at the Hacienda. They didn't look anything like the people you used to get in there, so I said hello and asked them what they were doing there.

Shaun said, 'We've got a band, Phil.' We had a spliff and a chat and I asked Mike Pickering to put them on. He got them their first proper gig, which was a local band night at the Hacienda. I think it was a Tuesday.

Despite this, the Mondays were going nowhere terribly fast . . . until the fateful day that Shaun met Bez.

The pair originally met in a pub in Eccles. Mark 'Bez' Berry had recently returned from a trip to Morocco, where he spent some time living in a cave with a man who made his own acid. Well, he'd had worse gaffs. Upon his return to Manchester, he was intrigued to hear all his pals talking about this 'Shaun Ryder' character. He was even more intrigued when everyone told him he should get together with Shaun because they would make a real pair. For one thing, neither ever had a spliff out of their mouth.

So it became frustrating when, for the next few weeks, every time Bez called at a pal's house he'd invariably just missed this 'Shaun Ryder' geezer by a matter of half-an-hour. Even though the pair were moving in the same close-knit, pot-smoking circles in Salford, they seemed destined to never actually meet. As they continued to miss each other by minutes, Bez and pals headed off on a drug-taking jolly down to Glastonbury, arrived three weeks early for the festival and camped up with some travellers for a few nights at a disused petrol station. They were offered everything from microdots to cups of tea made from puddle water, and had a ball until a dawn raid by police signalled it was time to go.

* * *

Back in Salford, Bez moved into his own flat in Eccles, and it was while he was celebrating moving in with a pint at the local boozer that he and Shaun finally met. The two Ryder brothers drove up in a bright yellow Ford Escort lovingly known as 'The Egg'. Introductions were made, and a friendship began.

That same day, Happy Mondays had just recorded 'Delightful', their first ever single, in a Stockport studio with Factory Records, A&R man Mike Pickering, who was later to become a leading Manc DJ and mainstay of handbag house chart band M People. Needless to say, the Ryder boys were very much up for a celebratory piss-up. Which, naturally, immediately ensued.

Shaun and Bez hit it off at once. Bez became a regular caller at Shaun and Paul's flat, and at their parents' house in nearby Little Hulton. Bez, who was living on his own after moving away from a housemate who went mad with a workman's angle grinder inside a rented flat, even had his Christmas dinner delivered by Shaun once, after Shaun's mum Linda took pity on him being home alone.

Nobody can precisely remember the first ever Mondays gig. Shaun says it was in 1984 at the Manchester Gallery, but others disagree. They had played a few in the early years at youth clubs and school halls. However, everybody remembers the famous gig in November 1985 when Bez got on stage with them at the Hacienda.

The Hacienda had long been the staple of Mancunian clubbing life. The Mondays had been going there since the early eighties, when the greatcoat and pointy shoe-wearing indie brigade ruled the roost. An ex-yacht showroom which had been bought by

Factory, the club still resembled a warehouse. The minimalist architecture, steel girders striped with multi-coloured chevrons, giant plastic strips hanging down from the main room entrance, and striped bollards around the dance floor made it look more like a factory floor than a place for off-their-trolley clubbers when the lights came up.

The Hacienda had played host to Madonna, who famously performed a wild and erotic routine on the dance floor while singing 'Like A Virgin', as well as everybody who was anybody in the music world. More importantly, it was where the Mondays – and half of Manchester – got their first taste of E.

Bez had been hanging around with the Mondays for a while. The first gig he watched them play was at Corbierres, a cellar bar off Cross Street, now long gone, but which doubled as a nightclub and held about 130 people. The Mondays had played longside a band called The Weeds, fronted by their favourite hairdresser. Bez had watched from the crowd after sharing pipes with Shaun and the gang backstage and was blown away by the whole experience.

So Bez accompanied the band to their Hacienda gig supporting New Order in November 1985. The gig was being broadcast on the coolest music show of the time, Channel 4's *The Tube*. Earlier that day, Bez and Shaun had necked some acid in a pub over the road. As their trips came on, the call came for the band to hit the stage. Shaun turned to Bez and told him he was coming on stage with them.

Bez disagreed; he didn't fancy it at all. But then Shaun called him a 'soft cunt'. This was the ultimate put-down. Bez was forced to prove he was no soft-arse and, in his chemically altered state of mind, strode with the band out on to the Hacienda stage (a stage which, incidentally, anyone who is anyone in Manchester has been sick on at some point in their lives). Bez froze, stood still and stared at the crowd like an LSD-bothered llama trapped in headlights. Shaun handed him a pair of maracas, the music started and the rest is history.

Phil Saxe had just started managing the band, and was backstage when the call came.

PHIL SAXE: I remember Shaun said, 'I want my mate on stage.' And I said it would look fucking stupid. He said, 'No it won't' and they went on stage together.

The interesting thing was that people used to wander in and out of the main rooms when bands were on, but that night the audience stayed where they were, looking at Bez and laughing. That was the exact point when I thought, Hey-up, THIS is interesting.

SHAUN: I decided to hand Bez a maraca that was lying about because it looked a bit better if he had something in his hand, something to play with, rather than just going out and dancing. I wanted him to shake it down the microphone, as well, because at that time there weren't computers making those kind of noises for you, which was always dead important to me.

CLINT BOON (Inspiral Carpets): I remember the first time I saw Bez, when he first became Bez. He went from being a mate who was just dancing, to being this icon. It was at the Hacienda; he had a pair of bug-eyed wraparound shades on, and he was dancing like an absolute freak. We were just laughing at him and then all of a sudden people started mimicking him. He had been hanging about with the Mondays for a long time, but on that night he just went on some different direction. I remember just looking at him and thinking, 'Fucking hell, he looks like one of the Velvet Underground.' He was going for it with his arms out and his tongue out; I thought, 'He's a proper star, he is.' It was the night Bez went from being a caterpillar to being a butterfly.

The fact that Shaun and Bez were both completely off their trollies when this legendary event happened was sort of ominous. Or maybe portentous is a better word. Either way, it was an apt chemical baptism for the new-born brothers of the chemical generation. This was just the start.

It was a few months later, during the recording of the 'Freaky Dancing' single, that Bez was officially made a member of the Mondays. New Order's Bernard Sumner had been brought in to act as producer as a favour to Phil Saxe. Bez had turned up with Shaun as usual, and stood in the corner to watch the session and the inevitable verbal batterings dished out from Shaun to the other members of the band, while he hung around and rattled his maraca as best as he could.

The band would launch into a tune and Bez would be transported back to that night at the Hacienda; the faces, the music, the acid, the rushes. The lights sweeping across the heads of the people on the dance floor, turning the whole club momentarily into an indecipherable sea of iridescent light. The eyes and teeth flashing from the cavernous depths. The arms punching the sky. Every note sent him spinning back to that joyous night and kept him longing for more.

It was on one of these days in the studio with Bernard that Manc photographer Kevin Cummins came to the studio for some publicity shots of the band. Shaun ordered Bez to get in on the photos, telling him: 'You're one of us now, dude. Freaky dancing – that's you.'

So why *did* Shaun insist on Bez joining the Mondays? With the gift of hindsight, Ryder now claims that he didn't parachute Bez into the band just because he was a buddy. Shaun reckons it was because he saw the charisma behind Bez's outlandish ways, and loved the way he created his own madness, just by himself. He also says he thought Bez would be a valuable asset in getting the band noticed.

He certainly wasn't wrong there.

SHAUN: I brought Bez in basically because there were no characters in our band except for me. The Mondays were pretty characterless really. Paul Davis, Mark Day and our kid could behave like three little clowns in real life, but they wouldn't use it as a stage presence or anything. They'd just shut up and stay quiet when they got up on stage. I was always into show business as well. Bez was a pal. I brought him on stage at the Hacienda to lift things up, because no other bands had anybody dancing with them. It was something different.

In those days, which were the Boy George days, we used to get A&R men coming down and they'd see us in our trainers, trackies, Adidas gear and side-partings. They'd say to us, 'You've got no image,' and we'd go, 'This *is* our image.' To us, in those days, flickers, or crew-cuts, and Adidas gear and trainer gear, that was an image, but these guys didn't see that. They wanted Duran Duran-type things. So Bez was brought on because he was a character and to do that image thing. To help us get recognised.

So was Shaun the mastermind plotting an unlikely and triumphant future for the band – or did Bez just get up on stage because he was off his tits on acid? In truth, nobody apart from those two knows. It suits Shaun that people think he had the vision to employ Bez as a wonderful gimmick who would get the Mondays noticed, and win them more column inches on account of their new in-house crazy loon. Shaun insists this is the true state of affairs, but others see it as him interpreting the past as he sees it now, rather than how it happened at the time.

TONY WILSON: The lead singer is always the face of the group. And the fact that there was this complete oddball, this very, very individualistic maraca player, was great PR as well. If you think about it, it's very weird.

But I think they were all characters. They were all personalities. Shaun forgets this. The reasons that he gives for getting Bez on board, and the digs at the others, are just post-event rationalisation.

Whatever the reasons for first drafting Bez in, though, he and Shaun inevitably became inseparable muckers and partners-in-crime as soon as Bez was ensconced in the band.

How to describe their bizarre, unique relationship? Well, if Shaun and Bez were comics, they'd be Laurel and Hardy. Shaun would be Ollie, headstrong and opinionated. Bez would be the hapless Stanley, the fatalist who just can't avoid getting into lumber because it's the lot of him and his blundering buddy. It's a wonderfully romantic notion to think of Bez as the hapless druggie who stumbled into stardom alongside his childhood best mate. Who, despite being musically inept became, purely by chance, the gangly, reaching, skeletal embodiment of the band and all they stood for.

In the early days, to the casual observer it seemed like the pair were living out some buddy movie together. They were Fonda and Hopper in *Easy Rider* (bad pun but you get the drift). They were the Two Musketeers, Mulder and Scully, *The Odd Couple*. They were most definitely *Men Behaving Badly* and, occasionally, Batman and Robin.

So Bez and Shaun were joined at the hip from the start – but the rest of the band didn't all take to the newcomer so easily. A few band members, particularly guitarist Mark Day and keyboardist Paul Davis, spasmodically gave Bez a hard time. It's true he did have the best job in rock'n'roll and that was something you could easily get jealous of. But the envious duo initially thought Bez was leeching off the Mondays and earning a crust from all their hard work.

'What does Bez *do*?' is a question that was – and still is – asked a lot by fans and critics alike. But more than anything he was the talking point of the band. He was what got the Mondays known faster than any other band in Manchester.

Rock'n'roll stunts like bands throwing tellies out of windows were old hat and boring as fuck. But when people saw Bez going mad for the tunes on stage they talked about him and told their pals about this fucking crazy man. So he quickly became a hero, and Cowhead and PD didn't like it. They saw it as him cashing in on their hard work. They were already on Factory Records when Bez joined them, so it was easy for some members to think they had already made it now they were rubbing shoulders with bands like New Order.

However, had it not been for Bez, things might have been a lot different. Bez wasn't just along for the ride. He had a purpose. He was born of necessity.

SHAUN: We had problems back in the early days with the money aspect for Bez. People couldn't see what he did for the band. I had Mark Day and all them lot saying: 'I play guitar, I do this and I do that, Bez isn't getting a part of that.'

But the thing is, Bez contributed to all the publicity. All the publicity is what made the band. All the wacky stories.

People wanted to interview him. They didn't want to interview Mark Day and hear him talking about A-minor, and what fucking strings he used on his Fender Stratocaster/Peavey amp rig. So Mark had to understand it was a team thing, people wanted to interview Bez, and that was just as important as what he was doing. Mark couldn't understand because he's narrow-minded, and that's why he's where he is now.

CHRIS MOYLES: Let's face it, Bez is a god. I remember the time when people were going, 'Well, what does Bez *do*?' and Shaun would defend him like he was the most important piece of the band. I thought that was great, and I liked the fact that they took no shit and did what they wanted to do. I think they were fantastic.

Shaun also recalls that in the early days, the Mondays had a novel way of acquiring new equipment:

SHAUN: I used to have this old wooden amp that we got from a place called Scan in Walkden, which at the time was the biggest superstore ever built in Manchester. It was built in the early seventies – it's a Tesco now. It was a huge place, with basically no security. It just had mirrors like in a normal corner shop, and you could walk into the place and walk out with tents and amps and records and everything, and that's what we did. I walked out with this big wooden box-amp designed to look like a crate, which was fucked and made everything echo and repeat. I used to get a microphone, mike it up and when you shook anything down it, it repeated and made weird noises. So I used to put percussion things in front of that and make noises which, when we first got into studios, never made it to the records because producers considered them odd.

The Mondays enjoyed a stream of indie hits, became music press darlings and were singled out for special attention by idiosyncratic Factory Records supremo Tony Wilson, who bigged them up to his American counterparts. Wilson decided that the natural next move was to take the band over to New York for New Music Seminar in 1986. This turned out to be the worst decision since Bob Geldof decided to start shopping for his own clothes.

The band arrived in NYC and, far from being overawed, vanished within five minutes of hitting Manhattan.

TONY WILSON: It happened on the very first day we took them to New York. We got out of Kennedy in a cab. I'd booked them in to the Chelsea Hotel as a joke, because the Chelsea is really fucking heavy, right. They came into Manhattan, their first time in America – for three of them, it was the first time out of England. They were in a cab with Phil Saxe, but the cab arrived at the hotel and there was only Phil Saxe in there. I asked, 'Where are the lads?' He said: 'They got out of the fucking cab. Sorry. The taxi stopped at Union Square and they just said, "This looks a good place," and jumped out of the cab.' So they've been in New York five-and-a-half minutes, and this is how clued they are to places, because they found the place to score drugs. No questions – there they were.

In fact, Shaun and Bez had jumped out of the taxi and made their way into Harlem to score some crack. At first they got ripped off, but continued undaunted deeper into the ghetto, where they thought all the 'real' people would be. And as luck would have it, these two English white boys wandering around the streets of Harlem came across a middle-aged black guy who invited them into his cellar to smoke.

Bez says the guy got spooked, so they left. Shaun says Bez spooked the guy so they left. Either way, as they left they ran into a local gang who were very much up for a fight. Bez tried to talk to them, but in his Bez-off-his-head scattergun style ended up accidentally spitting all over the leader of the gang, who then got miffed and pulled a gun on the pair.

SHAUN: It was just basically, right, when we were going over to New York, there was this thing in the papers about this new drug hitting America. Crack. As soon as we saw that, me and Bez were like, 'Fucking hell, we've got to try some of this. It's not just normal freebase cocaine, it's crack! Crack!' So as soon as we got off the plane, me and Bez went off to Harlem and places round there looking for this crack. And we found it, and went to this guy's crib, and we smoked with him in his crib and we were high as kites. Then when we came out we walked down the street looking for a taxi, and we got a bit lost and got surrounded by a load of different nationalities of people. They were all high on crack, and at the time the violence was starting to get out of hand in New York. It was really bad because of crack.

Bez was off his tits and he was drunk as well, and he was spraying out of his mouth as he was talking, so basically this guy thought I was spitting on him and pulled out a gun and shoved it in my eyeball. There was me high on crack and carrying a bottle of Budweiser in a brown paper bag, and as he put the gun to me I put the bottle to him, thinking 'Right, if he's going to shoot me, I'm sticking this in his eye.' The geezer had warned us three times, and I was saying, 'Listen, man, I don't know what you're talking about! Spitting?' I couldn't turn round, could I, and say, 'It's Bez, he always spits when he's drunk!'

So this guy was thinking it was me gobbing on him and Bez was right off his thing anyway.

Then right out of nowhere this dude who we'd been smoking with, and who we bought this gear off at his crib, appeared, even though we were about a mile away from his gaff. He fucking saved me life, really. He appeared out of nowhere, fucking took the gun off the kid and told him to fuck off. Then he told all the others to fuck off. He was a bit older than all these other ones, you know what I mean, and they obviously respected him because they did fuck off.

I wasn't scared at all, then the next day, right, when like me crack had come off and I realised that I'd had this gun stuck in my eye and everything, I just fucking got a panic attack.

TONY WILSON: Shaun and Bez finally came back to the hotel at three in the morning. We got them to the gig the next day, and they found some woman at the gig who was a co-promoter and a drug dealer – and that was the last we saw of them for that day until twenty minutes before the gig. She was a fucking nuisance she was anyway.

Shaun and Bez took to their new promoter/dealer friend very quickly. She'd taken the lads up to her apartment nearby and lined up some fat lines of coke for the pair while peeling off and performing a very erotic striptease show for them, before her friend joined her to make it a two-girl show.

SHAUN: Basically we should have been on the stage at the Limelight and she took me and Bez back to her apartment. She gave us loads of cocaine and her and her mate were undressing, kept coming in the room with less and less clothes, giving us more and more coke, you know what I mean. Then, the next thing, Bez said, 'I'm going to the shop to get some booze.' There's these two gorgeous chicks, one a boss at the Limelight. I turned around and said, 'Well, I'm coming with you.' And she and her mate just couldn't believe it, you know what I mean. And me and Bez were well coked up. So we went off and then we realised, 'Oh fuck, we've got to be on stage!' Me and him were right scruffy gets, and this model of a babe club manageress of that place, you know, had been coming on to us like that. She was well out of our league.

It was no surprise that their minds were blown when it came to the gig later that day. It was probably one of the Mondays' most infamous, off-it shows, with even PD, the keyboard player, having to move his stuff on to the floor so he could play lying down because he was so wankered.

The Yanks, however, were less than impressed with the show put on for them – although Tony Wilson, looking back, claims it was one of the band's greatest moments in terms of showing what they were about.

TONY WILSON: One of my proudest reviews ever was in the *New York Times* of the Music Seminar gig. The review said something like an English group was playing, called the Happy Mondays, 'who were so out of it that they couldn't stand up. So they didn't.' And that was the review I think. I particularly remember the fact that PD had to lie on the floor to play the keyboards. I thought that was great.

On the band's return to Britain, their debut album was released. They'd cut *Squirrel And G-man 24 Hour Party People Plastic Face Carn't Smile (White Out)* in London with John Cale, the former Velvet Underground musician. It wasn't fantastically received. Whereas Bernard Sumner had managed to capture the vibe of the Mondays in his recording sessions, Shaun says Cale, a reformed heroin addict, couldn't get his head around what the band were doing.

SHAUN: I think he thought that we sounded like shite. He didn't have the patience we needed and was being too adult about the whole thing.

Cale also couldn't handle the volatile nature of the Mondays, who would regularly resort to physical violence to resolve disputes in the studio. It wasn't uncommon for bottles and knives to be used. One rumour even has it that a band member was actually stabbed during these sessions, but no one seems to remember that.

> **GAZ WHELAN:** One night Shaun was doing my head in and I leaped out from behind my drum kit to crack him. Shaun's dad Horseman tried to break it up, but Shaun bit me on my fucking head. He was always scrapping, especially with PD. Once the fucker took five of us out with a metal pole while we were on stage in France.

The only person who didn't get any arguments from Shaun, the main protagonist, was Bez. The pair of front-cover buddies stayed pals through the whole Mondays career. *Their* big fall-out was to come, years later, in Black Grape.

Squirrel And G-man . . . was described by one critic as sounding like Joy Division jamming with Hot Chocolate in a brothel with a grizzled Steptoe on vocals. The Cale sessions were an inspired idea by Tony Wilson – Cale's name would carry some weight in the States – but they weren't about to launch the Mondays on to *Top Of The Pops*. That was still another two years and another album away.

The Mondays' notoriety steadily grew and they became increasingly feted by the music press, but it was with their next album, 1988's *Bummed*, that things really started to happen. *Bummed* was recorded in a studio in Driffield, a small East Yorkshire town whose only other claim to fame is that Chris Evans once broadcast his Radio One breakfast show there. They still talk about it in the pubs there. It's that sort of town.

The move to Driffield was yet another cunning Factory ploy to keep the band away from drugs. It was a waste of time on two counts. One, because they took their own narcotics with them, and two, because the man doing the production was none other than Joy Division guru and 'master chemist', Martin Hannett. Hannett had fallen out with Factory and had been threatening legal action, so it came as more than a little surprise to observers when the Mondays said they wanted him for their next album. The sessions were fuelled by Ecstasy which some pals of Bez had brought over from Amsterdam.

> **SHAUN:** Martin Hannett created this great drum sound with Joy Division, so we just thought, 'Let's try him.' We didn't really know much about producers, we just knew he was better for us at the time than Pick [Mike Pickering].
>
> And I've got to honestly say that was the one time I've ever worked with a producer who was more stoned and off it than I was.

It was Bez's contribution of the Es along with Hannett's production that led to the buzzing, psychedelic atmosphere of *Bummed* and marked a turning point in the Mondays' music. It is still considered by some to be the band's finest hour and features classics like 'Mad Cyril', 'Do It Better' and of course the anthemic 'Wrote For Luck'. The album reached number 59 in the charts and a relatively unknown DJ, Paul Oaken-fold, was brought in to remix 'Wrote For Luck'. He also changed the track's name to 'WFL'.

The result was an unforgettable anthem which despite a low chart position won an immediate follow-ing in the clubs of Manchester. It was a tune which was played on both indie and house nights, because it incorporated the beats and rhythm of house music along with the groove of the live band.

PAUL RYDER: It was the sound we had been looking for all along. When I first heard it I couldn't believe it. It was fucking fantastic, and all I could say was, 'Fucking hell.'

The Mondays had been playing low-key gigs in and around Manchester for over a year, supporting bands like James at the Ritz. Their own following, however, was growing. As was their legend.

TONY WILSON: I gave a speech to the Factory staff in the autumn of '87 saying, 'We've had a really good year and things are going well. But let's not get too full of ourselves – there's another musical revolution around the corner. It might not happen in Manchester, but keep your eyes open.'

I gave that speech to everyone, and at the same time one member of the Mondays, a group we'd signed eighteen months earlier, was standing on his own in the middle of the Hacienda dance floor waving his fucking arms in the air. Another two of them were selling these little tablets around the back. We were sitting right on top of the explosion.

The Mondays brought in and sold all the Ecstasy and Bez used to dance like he does on his own. They were the origins of the culture and quite rightly so – they were the origins of the music. The *Daily Telegraph* once wrote a piece about a Mondays gig at Wembley which said: 'Before we go on about the madness, the anarchy and the drug hysteria, which is all wonderful, let's not forget that the drummer and bass player of this group have changed British music forever.' Because it was Gary Whelan and Paul Ryder who adapted the rhythms of American house music to English rock. To punk, in fact.

The Stone Roses wrote great rock songs, but they weren't acid house. But people now remember them for 'Fool's Gold'. That's when they, Primal Scream and everybody else took one look at what the Mondays were doing and said, 'Oh right, wow!' and they put that rolling rhythm into their music. I've always said that 'baggy', as a musical term, is that rolling rhythm you find in those later Stone Roses and Primal Scream tracks.

It was obvious it was time for the new movement that became acid house. I'd seen these movements before as a kid and as a teenager, because I lived through punk. So I studied the process very closely, and by God I was aware of how it worked. I didn't forget how small it was when it started.

If you think *Hot* at the Hacienda started in April 1988, and that summer was the first Summer

Of Love, it's hard to imagine that in December 1988 we were putting on a rave in a swimming pool, advertising it massively, and having only 180 people turn up. A Guy Called Gerald and 808 State played. Nine months later you'd have had 3,000 people battering the doors down.

The precise cultural moment in which the United Kingdom was introduced to acid house, the moment which everyone thinks was a great breakthrough, was November 1989, when the Mondays and the Roses were both on the same edition of *Top Of The Pops*. Everyone forgets that in November 1988, when it was still almost nothing, New Order played 'Fine Time' on *Top Of The Pops* and Barney Sumner did Bez. Barney danced exactly like Bez. And the three thousand people in Manchester who knew about the Mondays saw Barney being Bez for the whole three minutes. The imagery of Bez was so potent that Barney could do it on *Top Of The Pops*. The rest of the country just thought, oh Barney's got a daft new dance. I always said Barney is the ultimate post-modernist performer, because when Barney's on stage doing that dance which looks like he's farting, what he's saying is I know that you know, that I know you know that I know I look like a prick. Suddenly there he was, and he was doing Bez. It was the first taste of acid house in Britain. That's how potent Bez's thing was.

'WFL' quickly became a defining anthem of the E-fuelled acid house scene, a club staple alongside classics like Black Box's 'Ride On Time' and 'French

Kiss' by Li'l Louis. The UK music scene's rules were being rewritten and the Mondays were right in the forefront of the changes.

Bez's influence carried on through the clubs and began to permeate mainstream culture. When the demos of Oakenfold's remix of 'Hallelujah' began to circulate round the clubs in early 1989, the Mondays became *the* band to follow. They helped prescribe the limits and the direction of acid house. The limits were nowhere and the direction was wherever they were going, which, more often than not, was to the Hacienda.

TONY WILSON: I remember in February 1989, suddenly there was now this thing in the club that nobody was putting their arms in the air while dancing to acid house like they'd used to in the beginning. It had become more horizontal with the arms, like the Ibiza thing, and the bandannas had all gone as well. I was talking to someone in the club about what a shame it was the arms had come down and the bandannas had gone, and he said, 'Oh, I knew that was going to happen.' I said, 'Oh?' He said, 'Yeah, I was in "acid corner" at the Hacienda in November and Shaun shouted at Bez, "Get your fucking arms down!" ' And that was that. It was another cultural moment. Shaun shouts at Bez to get his arms down, and a few weeks later everyone's arms are down. That's how cultural leaders work. He was beyond description.

FATBOY SLIM: To be honest, I think the Mondays were more important to non-dance music than to dance music. In those early days, they definitely set the standard of rock bands being into going out and clubbing. Rather than just saying, 'Right, let's sack the guitarist and become a dance band,' they said, 'Well, let's see how we can merge the two,' and worked with Oakenfold and Vince Clarke and people. But it was probably more important that they opened the door for rock acts to be allowed to use drum loops and work with dance producers, rather than the other way round.

I don't think they had that much effect on dance music because dance music always kind of had its own rules anyway. But before the Mondays, if you mixed rock and dance then all the rock fans were up in arms. They would boycott your gigs and have demonstrations outside, saying 'How can you do this?' I remember when I went from the Housemartins to making dance music, which is what I did before anyway, there were Housemartins and Smiths fans who wanted to lynch me.

After the Mondays did it though, with so much style and aplomb, it was suddenly allowed. I think the cross-pollination was definitely from dance music into rock. I don't think dance music changed its rules after that.

Looking back, I think the Mondays and Primal Scream set the precedent. But the Mondays were a) the first ones to do it, b) did it the best and c) were the ones who actually did it because they'd been hanging around in clubs listening to the music, rather than the A&R men saying I think you should work with this producer and get him to remix you.

When 'Hallelujah' was released on the 'Madchester Rave On' EP, in November 1989, things went ballistic for the band. The EP went Top 20 and led to the now legendary *Top Of The Pops* appearance alongside the Roses. 'Hallelujah' echoed perfectly the spirit of the age. In Berlin the wall dividing east and west had just come down, England were through to the World Cup, and Maggie Thatcher was on her way out.

Phil Saxe, meanwhile, stepped down as Mondays manager. He had taken the reins only as a favour to the band, and didn't feel able to dedicate the time to the band that he felt they needed as their fame grew. Now they needed a proper full-time manager and 28-year-old Nathan McGough, the son of sixties Liverpool poet Roger McGough, took on the job.

Then, in early 1990, the Mondays' third album, *Pills 'N' Thrills And Bellyaches*, produced by Oakenfold and his partner Steve Osborne, catapulted the band into the mainstream of British pop culture. The album had been recorded in Los Angeles – the band's first visit there. They stayed at the famous Oakwood apartments, and stories from that particular jolly vary from Bez nearly bedding Julia Roberts to Chris Quentin, aka Brian Tilsley from *Coronation Street*, breaking down in tears when they collared him in the BBC bar and took the piss.

SHAUN: We toured around the States before we went to cut the album. We'd been to New York a couple of times by then and visited a few places, but this was the first time that we'd stayed in one place for any length of time. We were there for a couple of months or something. The Oakwood apartments were full of porno actresses and things like that. A couple of our lads ended up shagging porno actresses. There were always parties and orgies going on. Obviously at the time there wasn't any E, apart from what the Brits had, and what we had brought over.

Chris Quentin was kind of snotty to us at first, all, 'Oh no not them,' and then ended up trying to suck up to us. He really ended up freaking out one night because we wouldn't let him pal around with us. We had a great time, though, in those apartments. We made connections for weed. And we had hire cars. Bez had about five accidents.

Pills 'N' Thrills And Bellyaches went straight into the charts at Number Four. It featured 'Kinky Afro', a testament to fatherhood and a gripe at Shaun's own old fella Horseman; 'Step On', a version of a John Kongos song which was recorded for an Elektra tribute album but which Shaun liked so much that he refused to let them use it, and the classic 'Loose Fit'. The album arguably represents the Mondays' musical high-water mark.

The party carried on all through the start of the nineties, with the Mondays' legendary hangers-on brigade growing and growing. *Pills 'N' Thrills* ... stayed in the charts for 28 weeks and won various awards for album of the year.

Late in 1990, however, *Melody Maker* revealed that Shaun was in treatment for heroin addiction. He had started messing around with the drug two years earlier during the John Cale studio sessions for the first album. The news came as no shock to the band, but to legions of fans who had associated the Mondays primarily with the heady, loved-up delights of Ecstasy, it came as a shock to hear their hero was now detoxing from the evil brown powder.

Tony Wilson was fully aware of the problems but was powerless to get Shaun off heroin. Shaun soldiered on, in and out of rehab, and the heroin became a steady fixture in his life. Friends saw it turn him nasty and sly.

And Shaun's new-found addiction was only one of a host of contributing factors which suddenly, at the height of their success, seemed to be conspiring to rip the band apart. Nathan McGough, the band's new manager, had told Shaun he was due a 50 per cent share of the band profits and PRS payments because he was the lyricist. Previously, the band had been roughly equal in their shares of profits. There were also further arguments about what Bez was entitled to, with the musicians, most notably PD and Moose, saying he wasn't getting any part of theirs because he didn't do anything.

An agreement was struck, but never set in stone, that each member should give Bez a one or two per cent cut of their PRS payments. They figured that this way, at least Bez would eventually get a pension and be able to pay his mortgage – but this arrangement soon went out of the window.

Trouble continued to dog the Mondays. Shaun, while still messing around with heroin, gave an MTV interview during which he joked about earning money as a young lad by selling his arse in Manchester for 50p a time. The next day, the headline in the *Daily Star* read: 'Happy Mondays Singer Confesses: "I Was A Rent Boy".' Shaun was livid and legal letters were exchanged. Lawyers told him he was in a strong position to claim damages for libel – until Shaun went on TV again and slandered the journalist who had written the story. The lawsuit was withdrawn.

The next negative event was far more damaging. Steven Wells from the *NME* journeyed to Manchester to interview the band for a cover feature. He had never been a fan of what he regarded as the Mondays' opportunistic and mercenary attitudes, and arrived with the apparent intention of stitching them up. Wells fired loaded questions about homosexuals at Bez and Shaun. Shaun was cagey but Bez answered honestly, if extremely naïvely, using the only language he knew.

In the following week's *NME*, Bez was quoted as saying he hated 'faggots'. This was clearly untrue, as the Mondays had numerous openly 'out' gay pals, and enjoyed drinking at The Rembrandt and various other bars on Canal Street, in Manchester's gay village. (Indeed, Shaun had told MTV that The Rembrandt was where he'd supposedly sold his arse!) Nonetheless, this time the damage was done. Bez's clumsy slip was picked up by the tabloids and caused a lot of bad feeling and resentment among their predominantly right-on and student audience, some of whom smashed Mondays records and posted them to *NME* in protest.

Things were getting worse. Relationships in the band were deteriorating by the day, and Factory Records were also in financial trouble. Pleased with the success of their musical protégés, Factory had embarked on a spending spree which included a revamp of their offices and fitting a zinc roof costing several hundred thousand pounds. They also invested in property and computers and spent an exorbitant amount on recording budgets for little-known artists. Their profligacy was typified when they bought an incredibly expensive conference table which was suspended by wires from the boardroom ceiling. It collapsed when the Mondays sat on it for a photoshoot.

Factory was struggling badly. It had been a year since *Pills 'N' Thrills* had been released and New Order were 'on a break' so there was no real money coming in. Then the property market collapsed and Factory's investments were suddenly worth zip.

Tony Wilson called a series of crisis meetings. It was decided that the answer was to get the Mondays to record another hit album. This was, indeed, a sensible solution, but there were two major problems: relations between band members were worse than ever, and Shaun was still struggling with his heroin addiction.

The events that happened next have passed into contemporary and pop culture folklore – and brought the curtain firmly down on the first incarnation of the Happy Mondays. Factory made a decision – born, one can only assume, out of desperation – to send the band to Eddy Grant's Blue Wave studios in Barbados. Paul Oakenfold and Steve Osborne, the winning team behind previous Mondays recordings, were tied up with other projects and unavailable for the sessions. So, with one eye on the American market, Factory drafted in the ex-Talking Heads/Tom Tom Club husband-and-wife team Chris Frantz and Tina Weymouth to produce the album. Tony Wilson now accepts that this was one of the biggest mistakes he ever made. Which is saying something . . .

TONY WILSON: I did an interview with Bez in Scotland quite recently and for the first time I publicly admitted that Chris and Tina were the wrong choice. Bez knew it. He said to me, 'Tina and Chris are brilliant, they were great. But their sound is the Tom Tom Club of the late seventies and early eighties. You should have found us the next sound.' And he's totally, totally right. Nathan and I failed the band – I have no doubts about that. Maybe we should have found them Danny Saber, I don't know, but we shouldn't have gone back. We should have found somebody else.

Yet the chosen producers were only a small part of the problem. One reason that Factory had chosen Barbados was that it was an island free from smack. Which was true. They thought that as there was no heroin, the album should be easy. To quote the fount of all knowledge that is the great unwashed Jim Royle: 'Easy my arse!'

The Mondays' problems began before they even got on the plane. Trish McNamara, Shaun's girlfriend at the time, dropped the bag containing Shaun's methadone at the airport and the bottle smashed on the floor. Shaun went ballistic as his brother ran around scooping it up into empty water bottles. Shaun had to filter his methadone through a pair of tights. But it was when the group arrived in the Caribbean that the trouble really began.

TONY WILSON: I remember Nathan McGough said to me, 'Let's send them to do it in Barbados because there's no smack there.' Yeah, great. Nobody bothered to tell us that it was crack fucking central, though.

Within minutes of arriving, Paul Ryder was being offered rocks while sunbathing on the beach close to the hotel. Naturally, it didn't take long for the good news to spread. Bez and Shaun were staying away from the rest of the band at the complex which housed the studios, partly because of the strained relations in the band, and partly so that Shaun would be close at hand when needed for the sessions.

BEZ: The recording might as well have stopped there and then.

Paul and, particularly, Shaun began to dedicate their days to getting hold of, and smoking, as much crack as possible. The already strained relationships within the group completely disintegrated. The band were rarely in the studio, and never there together. Shaun had written not one word of lyric.

Bez, meanwhile, developed a penchant for hiring and trashing cars. This wasn't deliberate; he was simply accident-prone. The number of cars written off during those few weeks in the sun is subject to dispute, and there's no point asking anyone in the band because they can't remember. Estimates vary between four and eight. Bez also managed to break his arm no less than three times in various boating and motor accidents.

TONY WILSON: There was a wonderful quote from Tina Weymouth, which was: 'The band caused terrible trouble the first afternoon they arrived. By the end of that afternoon all the maids were upset because they had taken the insides of all the toilet rolls to use as crack pipes.'

Her other great line was, 'I've lived through the seventies and the eighties, and I know a lot of people who've lived life on the edge, but I've never before met a bunch of people who don't even know where the fucking edge is.'

However, although nobody denies the drugs in Barbados were a huge problem, they weren't the only thing trashing the Mondays. Their attitude had changed. Their success and burgeoning media fame had affected them.

TONY WILSON: Everyone knows the stories about what happened to the band in Barbados. What they don't know, though, is that it wasn't just about the crack. Shaun went off the rails partly because he'd had this group, *his* group, for eight years and suddenly, after *Pills 'N' Thrills*, they were a famous group. So when they got out to the studio in Barbados, Shaun was doing his normal thing of 'You do that, Gary,' or 'You do that, Paul,' and suddenly everyone was saying, 'Excuse me, do you know who the fuck I am? I'm the drummer in the Happy Mondays, I'm a great musician and I do what I want!' They all stopped taking their lead from Shaun because they were all big and famous in their own rights. Or so they thought.

But obviously one of the reasons the band wouldn't do what Shaun said was because he'd got into crack, which is a shit fucking drug. Cocaine is a great destroyer of talent in any business – particularly the music industry. I can remember Alan McGee saying to me, 'Tony, Tony, you've got to sell the Mondays now because they're all going to die soon. They're all junkies.' And I said, 'What's wrong with junkies? It's not an issue. They can create great art.' I think heroin's a shitty drug and it makes you behave very badly, but it doesn't rob your creativity. The great founder of Atlantic Records, Ahmet Ertegun, said most of his great artists were junkies, had been for 25 years, and had spent 25 years giving him platinum albums. But cocaine takes your talent. It robs you.

Weymouth and Frantz were distraught, and had no idea how to handle these wild-eyed Mancs who were wreaking havoc all over their recording plans – and the island of Barbados. Phone calls went back and forth to the Factory offices in (appropriately) Charles Street, Manchester, with the latest reports.

Then things turned really ugly. Shaun phoned Factory when the cash ran out and threatened that if Wilson didn't send the band a five-figure sum immediately, he'd destroy the master tapes of the album so far. Wilson panicked and re-mortgaged his house to meet the ransom demand. He then had to fly over to LA on business, where he got another call from the studio begging him to stop off in Barbados on his way back and try to sort out the mess. It had gone well beyond Horseman's and Nathan's control.

TONY WILSON: I thought Bar bados was just off the coast of Florida, so I was all ready to go. Then I took a look at the map and no, it wasn't off Florida, it was just off fucking Venezuela.
Suddenly I realised there was no way I could do it. It was impossible. I had to be back in Manchester in two days' time, so I didn't go. And if anyone ever asks me, 'Do you have any regrets in your life?' I've only got one regret in my entire fucking life and that is that I didn't go to Barbados. I couldn't have solved the mess, mind, but I would have liked to have fucking seen it.

The night I decided not to go to Barbados was the night that someone heard a noise and managed to stop Shaun as he was opening the back doors of Eddy Grant's studios. He had a van outside and was loading the fucking sofa into the van to take down to town and sell it for crack.

That's my boys.

The album which resulted from the anarchic Barbados sessions, *Yes Please*, was finally finished and released in October 1992. It reached number 12 in the charts, but was slammed by the critics as anodyne, uninspired and pedestrian. A shambolic UK tour followed, during which the Ryder brothers were both incapacitated by dreadful smack habits and the band weren't even on nodding, let alone speaking, terms.

The personal lives of the individual Mondays continued to flounder. Paul Ryder's heroin addiction led to a split from Astrella and his kids. Then the inevitable finally happened. Factory Records went under.

The demise of Factory was the beginning of the end for the band. The nail in the coffin, though, was entirely of Shaun's making. For a short while, their future had looked brighter. Nathan McGough had persuaded EMI to offer the band £1.7m for a five-album deal. The deal was due to be signed in the label's Manchester office in February. Shaun was to receive approximately £200,000 as his share of the advance – but was then informed by EMI that they were to cut the figure to less than £20,000. They had been convinced by keyboardist Paul Davis that he, and not Shaun, was the main songwriter and band leader.

SHAUN: That really got on my tits. We were dealing with EMI and they rang me up and said, 'We've heard Paul Davis is leading the band.'

I said: 'Well he isn't, but what if he was?'

They said: 'Well, we're going to have to drop the price we're offering you.'

And I went, 'Well, why?'

They said, 'Because Paul Davis is the main man, not you,' and I nearly choked on my own fucking spit. I said 'You WHAT?'

They said, 'Well, we've been talking to Paul, and we think Paul is the main player.'

I just said, 'Nah, you're off your head there.' Because, you see, PD could look like a sensible person but I thought he was a freak. He lives in this Walter Mitty world, big time. PD had been giving all these interviews, saying, 'I'm doing this and I'm doing that, I got this show set up and I wrote that song,' and the EMI people believed him because he looked quite straight and he acted straight. He looked the part, whereas I looked fucked half the time.

See, I'd purposely taken the role of being the bad boy of rock because it helped the image. Everyone has got an image. The Rolling Stones were bad boys, Jagger was Mr Sex and Richards was Mr Drugs. Johnny Rotten was spitting and sniffing glue or whatever – and we had our theme. It was our image – we used what little we'd been given, learned to exploit it. So as soon as we were given this druggie rock'n'roll image, just for liking a spliff, then straight away we decided to turn it to our advantage. But these EMI people believed Davis because he looked so straight whereas I got all this shit thrown at me, with everyone saying I was a nutcase.

I couldn't believe these people all believed PD rather than me, and really thought he was the leader of the band, but then I just thought, right, well, fuck you then. I walked out of the deal.

Shaun had arrived hours late for the EMI meeting and just before he was due to sign on the dotted line along with the rest of the band, excused himself from the room, saying he was going to buy some Kentucky Fried Chicken. He did, indeed, go to the KFC on Oxford Road with his girlfriend Trish. He bought a family-size bargain bucket and sat in his car interspersing chewing on a drumstick with chasing the dragon.

He didn't, however, go back to the meeting room.

The band felt Shaun had let them down and Shaun felt the band had let him down. Bez, as always, was on the side, looking on.

TONY WILSON: The best way to make sense of the end of it all is, don't think of the Mondays as a band – think of them as a gang. Shaun's main crime was that he was the leader of the gang and he kept letting his gang down. The final let-down – even though I think he was probably right to do it – was going for a Kentucky when EMI were going to give them nigh-on a million pounds.

If you've got a gang you have to explain what you're doing to the gang, not just walk away and let everything fall apart. I had the experience of Factory going bankrupt. Everything was falling apart, but I was still in love with a single the Mondays had recorded, 'Sunshine of Love'. I thought it was a wonderful song. I didn't think it would turn our fortunes around but I just wanted to get it out.

So to make a video for it, I borrowed £200 from here and £200 from there. I borrowed a grand altogether. I also blagged some crewtime and cameras, and the whole purpose of this was to get a video for this Happy Mondays song. And Shaun Ryder wouldn't get out of bed to do it. Maybe he wasn't in my gang, but I was in his gang – and I was very honoured to be there, at the end of the day.

SHAUN: After I walked out on the deal, I kept my mouth shut. PD was giving interviews, saying, 'Yeah, I wrote all the stuff,' and so on, and I said nothing. I didn't talk to the press for two years. I had the biggest laugh of my life, though, when everything they tried to do failed.

You'd think those bigwigs in the music business would know better. They invent these scams and crazies, these made-up personalities, 'He has 90 shags a night' and stuff like that . . . and then they believe an idiot like PD. They said, 'Paul Davis is the main player.' And I was like, 'Well listen, kiddo, if you want to believe this you believe it, but I'm going. Ta-ta to the fucking lot of you.'

A week after Shaun Ryder went out for a Kentucky Fried Chicken, EMI withdrew their offer to the band.

There was interest from other record labels, but by now Shaun had irredeemably fallen out with the rest of the band. He regarded them as being just in it for the money now, considering pension plans more important than making good music. In short he saw them using Happy Mondays as a vehicle to everything he started the band to get away from.

The Mondays' first career had been a nine-year ride of rock'n'roll excess, drugs, women and fights. The band had become synonymous with hedonism and debauchery. However, the defiant, punky dynamic of 'had nothing, got nothing, want nothing' which made them special had been overtaken by greed and self-importance.

It was the final nail in the coffin and the band split. Happy Mondays were dead.

2. WHAT NOW FOR SALFORD'S LOST SON?

Shaun blows chunks in back of car, dies. Drinks oxtail soup from vase. Too-Nice Tom saves Shaun from suicide, Sport starts 'Talking Straight', Shaun sticks Posh Spice up his jumper.

The immediate aftermath of the Mondays split was messy and bloody. For the first few weeks, Mark Day and Paul Davis waged a vendetta against Shaun in the national tabloids and local press. They claimed they'd rather go on the dole than work with him again. PD promptly did so, while Cowhead had one last stab at a career in music before leaving the music biz and starting a job selling books door-to-door.

Shaun's bass player brother Paul, meanwhile, underwent therapy to help him off heroin and back into everyday life after living through the sort of excesses which make Keith Moon look like a shandy drinker.

There were also legal wrangles as it was sorted out who was owed what, for what. The band members kept their distance from each other, with only Bez and Shaun remaining pals through the bust-up. A few of them worked on other music projects in Manchester, but it was to be six years before certain members of Happy Mondays spoke to each other again.

Shaun Ryder, meanwhile, went into media hibernation. He co-wrote soundtracks for a couple of movies, Jackie Chan's *Supercop* and Robert DeNiro's *The Fan*, and made a guest appearance on a 1994 single by Manc band Intastella, which saw him wearing a dodgy whistle on the cover of *Melody Maker*.

Otherwise, though, nothing was heard of Shaun for two years. It seemed as though he'd vanished off the face of the Earth.

Then, in 1995, he re-emerged in style.

Shaun had teamed up with various musicians including Kermit, a rapper from Manchester's semi-legendary Ruthless Rap Assassins, and Paul Wagstaff (aka Wags) from local band Paris Angels, to form Black Grape. Together with producer Danny Saber, Black Grape recorded *It's Great When You're Straight . . . Yeah!*, an album of riotous rhythms which namechecked Jesus, the Pope, Batman and the Nazis.

Shaun said that he thought *It's Great When You're Straight . . .* was the album that the last Mondays record, the wretched *. . . Yes Please!*, should have been. It went straight to Number One in the album chart – a second coming that the Stone Roses, the Mondays' main Manc rivals, could only dream of.

SHAUN: The Black Grape comeback was brilliant – but I worked at it. Hard. People think I started Happy Mondays in the early eighties and then in 1993 sacked the Mondays, spent a couple of lazy years on the dole and then suddenly came up with Black Grape. They think I did nothing for two years and then suddenly just popped up with this new band.

But basically for those two years I'd been working on material, putting a band together, putting my team together, getting all these people that I wanted to work with, getting the music, the style, and doing movie themes and scores.

To the punter I just appeared again. For them, it was like 'Wa-hey! You're back!' But to me I'd never been away. I wasn't like the fucking shopkeeper out of *Mr Benn* – Boom!, as if by magic I appeared again. I was working every single fucking day.

Two days after the Mondays finished, me and Kermit went on a trip. We went to America, made music together and met movie soundtrack people. We were constantly working so that two years later we could just pop up with this Number One album.

But yeah, what made Black Grape so good was that we made it look so easy.

Black Grape went out on tour, with Bez once again freaky dancing alongside the band. When the tour ended, however, Bez walked out on the group. The reasons were shrouded in mystery at the time – but turned out to be money-based. Shaun felt that while he had learned a lesson from the collapse of the Mondays, Bez hadn't.

SHAUN: Basically me and Bez had a big fucking falling out because when we got Black Grape together we sat down and said, right, we're making no more mistakes like the Mondays did. There's going to be no more us paying for everyone to party, no more untold gangs of people towing along, no more extravagance. That was our plan.

But twelve months into Black Grape, we went from Bez needing three Es every gig to Bez needing ten Es every gig. Then he needed Ultrafuel, an expensive athletes' drink which cost us £100 a night. It wasn't like bodybuilding drinks where you put weight on, it was proper energy-giving stuff that costs a fortune. And he was getting this drink in, and then giving it away to everyone because he was off his head!

Bez would get off his napper and start saying to people, 'Taste this, taste this, have a drink of this,' and people would come in the dressing room and he'd pour it out. They'd have a taste, and they didn't realise that when you pour one cup of that shit out it's £10 and people would have a taste and then spit it out.

So Bez would in a night get rid of all the stuff that was supposed to last him through a whole tour, then the next morning he'd be saying, 'I'm not going on stage if I haven't got any Ultrafuel.' So that'd be another £100. Plus we were paying for all his Es as well, and Bez would have twenty hangers-on every night thinking it was a big free-for-all. So we had a big fall out. I said, 'Look, we lost a load of shit on the Mondays through this sort of craziness. I'm not paying for it any more. It's not coming out of band money. If you want it, you pay for it.' So we had a big row over that.

And Bez was smoking loads of crack again and being totally unreasonable. He was fighting, his temper was going, and he was threatening everybody – well, not us, but threatening business associates. The only decent thing he did was when he punched out Nik Nicholl who was our manager at the time. But even though, yeah, we all wanted Nicholl to be punched out, you can't go around punching managers. You know, you just can't. You might want to but you can't.

Bez punched Nicholl and we all silently agreed with him, but his temper was gone, he was smoking that much crack that nothing was getting through to him. He decided he was leaving. So we went, 'See ya then. Bye bye.' This happened a few times, and after a day we'd ring him up and say, 'Come on, come back, forget it,' but then one time we didn't. He was cracked out of his head, we couldn't get through to him and he was totally unreasonable. So he left the band and that was that.

Plus I was paying Bez's mortgage for him, £300 or £400 a month. I paid it out of my own money for twelve months. Then he started moaning about money and things like that at me and I'd say, you know, look, I'm paying your mortgage for you. Bez's big mistake was that he saw all the money he made out of the band as money to be thrown away. He kept hold of the money he made through his other ways, but he just spunked all the band money right away.

Bez used to divide his business up into two halves. There was the entertainment business and the, erm, other business. There'd be these other business people who'd say, 'Here you are Bez, there's a few grams of that to shift, or a couple of ounces of that,' and he'd pay them right back. But he'd pay them back out of band money, which at the end of the day was my money.

Bez would do my head in. He'd be saying to these cunts, 'Yeah, here you are Bozzo, Tozzo and

Twazzo, here's an 'undred tickets for ya.' That was costing us. We were paying for them tickets. So that's what it was all about. That's what the big fall out was about. Plus he was smoking way too much stone.

And Bez's departure wasn't the only problem eating Black Grape in 1996. Shaun was becoming increasingly dissatisfied by the band's husband-and-wife management team of Nik and Gloria Nicholl, who operated under the name of Nicholl and Dime. Nicholl and Dime had been recommended to Shaun by Gary Kurfirst, the owner of Black Grape's label Radioactive.

SHAUN: They were put in touch with me through Gary Kurfirst, just after the split with the Mondays. Now, I was under the impression Gary was our manager and they were just working with us. Obviously he couldn't manage us properly because he owned the label, and that would mean a conflict of interests.

So Kurfirst put forward Nicholl and Dime to manage me and I agreed because I wanted to get an album made. Plus, all the money from the Mondays had been frozen while we resolved who was owed what for what. There were bills for tour buses, concert equipment and whatever else, so everything was frozen until all that was sorted out.

I needed some cash and the only way to get that cash was to make an album, but I never realised how much money I was agreeing to pay Nicholl and Dime. So I sacked them in 1996 because I didn't like the way they did things.

Shaun accused Nicholl and Dime of serious mal-practice when dispensing with their services. They, in turn, launched a lawsuit against him for loss of earnings. The affair and its repercussions were to dog Shaun Ryder for the next four years.

Meanwhile, the now Bez-less Black Grape released their second album, *Stupid, Stupid, Stupid*, at the end of 1997. It was greeted by mixed reviews, unlike the adulation awarded its predecessor, but still went gold and made the Top Ten. Despite this, the band was being riven by the same kind of tensions which had eventually sounded the death knell for Happy Mondays.

Kermit was the first Black Grape casualty. The rapper fell out big time with Shaun after Ryder gave an interview to Dave Simpson, of *Melody Maker*, during which he bizarrely claimed that he'd watched Kermit injecting smack into his knob (Kermit's, not Shaun's). A subsequent rare apology by Shaun was to no avail, and Kermit left in a huff with another Black Grape cohort, co-vocalist Carl 'Psycho' McCarthy, to set up a group called Man Made, managed by Black Grape tour manager Anthony 'Muzzer' Murray.

Shaun now claims that Psycho had developed a rampant ego problem as a result of being caught up in the sudden success of Black Grape.

SHAUN: Muzzer had taken over managing Carl and Kermit. We got a proposal for Black Grape to go to Australia. It would have sold us shitloads of records over there. Carl and Kermit were getting a good percentage of record sales by this time. But the wage Carl wanted for going to Australia was exactly the same as the budget for the whole fucking tour, including taking the equipment!

Muzzer was saying, 'My artists are going nowhere until they get what they want.' I said, 'How can I pay your one artist the same as the whole budget for a whole band, all the fucking roadies, all the trucks, lights, everything?' It was ridiculous. But Carl by this time thought he was great and decided to take Muzzer's advice. So we never got to Australia.

In this business it's amazing what people believe if you tell them. Someone tells someone they're the next Elvis and before you know it they're running around acting like they are.

Shaun became pissed off with the whole affair and made off with about £150,000 from the last Grape tour to buy a farmhouse in Ireland where he went to spend time with his partner Oriole Leitch, the daughter of sixties folk icon Donovan. Bez, who had bought a house with his long-term girlfriend Debbie Faulkner in a quiet Derbyshire village near Glossop, was outraged by this development.

SHAUN: I was in Ireland and Bez was phoning me and shouting and threatening me. It was weird. For years I was his mate and I used to split our money in half and even paid his mortgage. But then he started going on at me: 'You took £150,000 to buy a house.' Well, so fucking what?

I thought it was about time I took something for my fucking self. And because Bez was being unreasonable he couldn't see that. I'd always looked after everybody else, including him. At the end of the day I had my family and I was making a new life.

At the time Bez thought I was being a twat, taking that money to buy my house. But I'd looked after everybody else for long enough, and basically, and I'm not being big-headed, if it wasn't for me none of them lot would have existed. Now that's a very big-headed thing to say, but it's quite true. Granted, if it hadn't been for Bez, on another level, we wouldn't have got all the publicity we got. It was teamwork and that's how he should have seen it.

But it wasn't until Bez stopped smoking the crack and got his shit together that he realised he'd been a bit of an idiot.

Black Grape was now reduced to the nucleus of Shaun and producer Danny Saber, and it was no surprise when the band split. Shaun was tired of the bitching, the back-biting, the touring and the whole lifestyle. What had begun as fun had turned sour. Relations between the band members were so strained and tense you could pluck them.

In December 1997, Black Grape's pre-Christmas tour was coming to an end. The band played Glasgow Barrowland, and the next night were due to round off the tour at Doncaster Dome. However, in the early hours of the morning, a pissed-off Shaun simply decided that he'd had enough.

SHAUN: By the end, Black Grape had got really bitter and twisted. It came to an end because I found myself boxed into a corner, just like in the

Mondays, where people took everything for granted – what you did, what you said, your whole personality. Everything got took for granted. Familiarity breeds contempt, and the people I worked with were now so familiar I felt nothing but contempt.

What happened was we'd got paid for the last gig that we did. It wasn't supposed, officially, to be our last gig, but I suddenly realised that all these people were taking me for granted. They had no respect for me. What I was doing had just become like working in a factory.

So one morning I woke up, and all these people I'd introduced to the business and who became tour managers, or managers, or publishers or whatever – I just woke up and thought bollocks to the lot of them. So I took the petty cash they all had in their bags, which was a couple of thousand pounds which had basically been earned by me. I put the money into my bag, gave it to my mate G-man, and we went off at seven in the morning.

Muzzer, the tour manager, used to sleep wrapped around the bag of money, so I left him a note at reception saying, 'Don't worry. Your money hasn't been robbed, I took it.' It was my money so we took it and went off.

It basically came down to the fact that I didn't want to be manipulated by some twats. I only ever wanted friendships. Money, and power, and shit like that I didn't want. But we'd all started off as friends and ended up as business acquaintances. By the end we weren't having a nobble, we were having meetings.

I lived with the money for a few weeks. I had Ireland, but also at the time I was having problems with Oriole so I couldn't go back there. In the end I just decided to make a clean break from everything.

I was on a bummer. I hadn't really had a break for the last ten years, and I decided I needed a break. I'd got to 35 years old and I thought it was about time I reinvented and rewrote my life.

Shaun decided he'd had enough of band life. He was getting old, and life on the road was taking its toll. He was also still dabbling in class A drugs and decided it was time to get clean, which, in retrospect, is rather like a leopard deciding to go for the striped look this summer.

Shaun packed his bumbag and checked in to London Bridge Hospital, south-east London. He paid £8,000 to have naltraxone implants in his stomach. Naltraxone is a chemical which gives an allergic reaction to heroin and thus helps to induce withdrawal. This time, possibly for the first time ever, he was genuinely trying to detox and kick his smack addiction.

However, as with all addicts, Shaun knew he would need constant care and attention if he were to stay on the straight and narrow. He upped sticks to the east Lancashire market town of Burnley where he moved in with clean-living film-maker and boxing trainer 'Too Nice' Tom Bruggen.

SHAUN: I went to Burnley because when I came out of London Bridge Hospital and I'd had the implants planted inside my stomach I needed some discipline. I needed to be in the right place with the right person. Tom decided that he'd take me on and help me through my detox. It's supposed to be this magic cure which costs £8,000 – they black you out for 24 hours and you withdraw while you're asleep, then they put these implants in you. But when you wake up you need some aftercare. Mine was at Tom's, which happened to be in Burnley.

'Too-Nice' Tom has truly earned his nickname. He's the genuine real-life embodiment of 'Brilliant', the *Fast Show* character who bounds around the world in a woolly hat and anorak finding the best aspect to everything. His glass is always half-full, and more. Even holding a conversation with Tom is weird. You expect that at any moment now he's going to start striding round the room shouting something like: 'Aren't mums brilliant! It's a good job they're all different though, otherwise you wouldn't know which house to go to for your tea!'

Yes, Tom Bruggen is one of the most friendly, affable people you could ever meet, despite – or because of – the fact that he doesn't drink, smoke or do drugs. He can talk the hind legs off a centipede and has one of the most incredible minds for remembering facts and figures (either that, or he's a top blag artist who makes them all up on the spot).

Tom had bravely volunteered to supervise Shaun's intended recovery. He'd known him for some years, and had been the man behind the Black Grape video documentary, *The Grape Tapes*. The duo had already started to write a film, and that was regarded as the way forward for the pair as a team. The movie was to be the new focus for Shaun.

So at 7 a.m. on Monday 13 January 1998, Tom collected Shaun from London Bridge Hospital. Ryder had been out cold for 24 hours under a general anaesthetic and was battered and bruised from nurses trying to restrain him for his own good as he cold turkeyed after years of substantial heroin abuse.

One fact soon became clear to both Shaun and Tom. Coming off the drugs, Shaun was in a state far worse than any he had ever got into while taking them. He was prescribed a vast combination of uppers and downers in massive doses to get him through the next few weeks. And as the anaesthetic began to wear off Shaun found himself in Tom's car, heading up to Burnley. He promptly threw up all over it.

Shaun's mind was blasted and he didn't know which way was up. He was a mental wreck, and as he came round in the back of Tom's Renault his first instinctive reaction was to blot out the pain and the anxiety with as many downers as possible. Shaun was firmly buckled in to the heroin detox rollercoaster ride to hell, and he was taking poor Too-Nice Tom with him.

TOO-NICE TOM: I went and met Shaun post-Naltraxone op. He was paranoid, sick and in a trance. There were tears. As we left the hospital together there were warnings and double warnings from the medical staff that he shouldn't drink, smoke or medicate above or below what he had been prescribed for the next three months.

Then the next thing I knew Shaun was dead. As far as I could tell he was dead, in the back of my

Renault. There was sick all over the seat and sick over me. He had taken over twenty high-dose capsules of Temazepam, which was twenty times his daily dose.

I raced home at 120mph on the motorway and called the doctor straight away. He said the overdose would kill him and told me to call an ambulance. Then Shaun came to, and he was right off on a trip. He was hearing voices and staggering around, protesting. I carried him to bed and he asked me to stay with him in case he died. He was very afraid of death.

When he came around again he wanted the amphetamines that had been prescribed for him to counter the effects of the sleeping tablets. Before I could stop him he took half a week's prescription in one go, which is enough speed to launch anyone else into orbit – and then drifted off to sleep.

The days that followed were nothing short of a living nightmare, for Tom and his heavily pregnant wife Di as much as for Shaun.

On the second day of withdrawal, in a state of utter terror, Shaun begged Tom to kill him, before falling down the stairs. Later the same day, as the voices and the mind-tricks of heroin withdrawal became too much, he tried to end it all by throwing himself from an upstairs bedroom window. He made a run for the window only to be rugby-tackled by Tom before he could make it. Tom wrestled Shaun to the floor and held him there until he became calm again and slipped back into unconsciousness.

TOO-NICE TOM: Shaun actually asked me to kill him. He was in a very bad way and he seemed to have superhuman strength. When he tried to throw himself out of the window it was all I could do to get him to the floor.

As well as sleeping pills, Shaun had been prescribed the drug Buscopan for stomach cramps, an anti-spasmodic for diarrhoea, Prozac for mood swings and amphetamines to get him out of bed. On top of that, Tom had to meet local dealers to get hash resin for Shaun on a regular basis.

The normally equable Tom was stuck with a madman, and frequently found himself reduced to tears as he tried to cope with Shaun day in and day out. The harrowing experience took its toll even on Tom's equilibrium, as illustrated by the recollections he has of these dark days.

He remembers that Shaun made eleven visits to the toilet while watching *Boogie Nights*. He burned 117 holes in the carpet during the first week alone, and watched *Trainspotting* eleven times – consecutively. He drank oxtail soup from a flower vase, and cooled his chips in the fridge before eating them.

As Shaun withdrew ever further into himself, he spent his days wrapped in a sleeping bag, his nose inches from the screen of a massive 50″ television where he'd stay for 24 hours watching movies like *Kelly's Heroes* and *The Jackal* from the local video shop. A traumatised Tom even took Shaun to a psychotherapist in Preston, who rapidly diagnosed the singer as a paranoid schizophrenic/manic depressive.

It was six weeks before Shaun Ryder began to approach anything nearing reality. They were the longest six weeks of his life. However, slowly and painfully he began to re-emerge from his massive slump. At last he began to dare to think that the worst was over – and to look forward.

> **SHAUN:** I think it helped that Tom's a boxing trainer and he gave me a bit of discipline. Otherwise somebody who comes off methadone after fifteen or sixteen years is going to basically just lie in bed. When I came out of hospital I was initially prescribed amphetamines which were equivalent to about two or three grams of speed a day. That was just to get me out of bed and to the toilet and back.
>
> So I needed some proper discipline. I'm quite a strong-minded person anyway. I would probably tell anyone else 'Fuck off, I'm staying in bed, I'm not getting up until 5 o'clock.' So we had to invent this routine which was quite hard and incorporated quite a lot of running, jogging and walking up hills. And taking pure Dexedrine.

So Ryder stayed with Tom and Di while he got straight and worked on a script for a movie called *Molly's Idle Ways*. This was about two girls who lived over the top of a gym, and the script cast Shaun as a drug-taking rent boy who gets to have sex with the leading lady. He found himself looking forward avidly to his new thespian career.

Once the script was complete Shaun and Tom began casting. Page Three girl Hayley Atherton agreed to be Molly. Shaun approached Radio One's Jo Whiley to play a pregnant lesbian mother, and Tom tried to involve one of the Gallaghers, to Shaun's disapproval. Sadly, funds dried up before the movie went into production, but it may still appear at some stage in the future. Talks are still underway.

As one door closes, though, another one swings open and bangs you in the bollocks. Shaun's career took a very bizarre turn when a visitor called at Too-Nice Tom's house – Tony Livesey, the managing editor of the critical acid bath of British pop culture known as the *Daily Sport*. Livesey went to visit Bruggen, one of his best friends from college years, in Burnley, and was introduced to Shaun there. Although Livesey had never been a huge Happy Mondays fan, he was impressed that Ryder was staying at his friend's house, and mentioned the meeting to his colleagues when he returned to the paper's offices in Manchester.

It was at that point that a light came on over the head of Marc Smith, the *Daily Sport*'s, er, sports editor. The bald-headed Smithy knew Ryder from Manchester, where he'd DJ'd at various clubs in the acid house years. The 1998 World Cup was about to begin, and Smithy suggested asking Shaun to write a review of the various football singles that had just been released.

In many ways, the *Sport* seemed a perfect employer for Shaun. He's a self-confessed pervert, with a wit which is matched only by his ability to swear like a fucking trooper. I myself worked for the *Sport* for two years, and while I'm not claiming all the people who read it are perverts, I know for a fact that some of the people who write it are, and proud of it they are, too! And maybe a publication which prides itself on the number and variety of female nipples it can squeeze into a 38-page edition is a natural home for the writing talents of the man who's been credited with single-handedly inventing lad culture.

So on 9 June 1998, Shaun made his debut in the *Daily Sport* reviewing football records. The battle raging in the charts at the time was between Skinner and Baddiel's 'Three Lions '98' and Fat Les's splendid 'Vindaloo'. Shaun had himself released a football song called 'England's Irie' with Black Grape back in 1996, and seen it lose out on sales to the 1996 version of 'Three Lions' – which meant he still harboured a grudge against Skinner and Baddiel.

The column was written in the week the English FA were meeting to choose their World Cup theme tune. When it appeared it was clear that this was the start of a beautiful relationship.

VINDALOO – FAT LES

Next time Keith Allen comes up to Manchester and wants a blow job off me he can f*** off, 'cos he never put me in his video.

What a big tune it is, dudes. Brilliant, absolutely fantastic, it's going to be massive and Number One, a lot bigger than Keith's knob . . . and that's a good job.

It won't just be a World Cup anthem, it will be the song on the lips of every lager lout invading the Mediterranean this summer. The FA need a kick between the legs for not getting him involved in an official version because he knows what Joe Public wants to hear in football songs.

Tiny penis Allen co-wrote 'England's Irie' with me before Euro '96 and also penned 'World In Motion', which is the muvva of footie songs.

This is certainly the song all the boys will be singing in the pub if England lift the World Cup. The video is almost as good as the tune, ripping the piss out of The Verve's 'Bittersweet Symphony'. I'm sure Richard Ashcroft saw the funny side though.

The only sad thing about it, though, is Keith got his idea to pen 'Vindaloo' after hearing Fulham fans chanting 'Na-na, na-na, na' while watching them play Bristol City.

At least he never got Kevin Keegan singing the chorus. If Kev's voice is as bad as the players he's bought for Fulham, no record company would release it.

ON TOP OF THE WORLD – ENGLAND UNITED

When I heard it I couldn't think of a worse football song ever, but after having spent a week in the car having it banged down my ears by wonderful Radio One, I dig it.

I love Ian McCulloch and the Bunnymen, but this is a feel-good tune that will grow on everyone as the World Cup goes on. It's patriotic, throat-choking emotional stuff that will tear at the chords of the heart as England march to the World Cup final.

THREE LIONS '98 – SKINNER AND BADDIEL AND THE LIGHTNING SEEDS

I'd prefer a blonde chick, a cigarette and a wank to this song – that's my three lions!

I hated the fucking thing from the first time it came out, because I thought 'England's Irie' was a much better football record. Like the rest of England I've been brainwashed by this, and now it's one of those songs just like 'Two Little Boys'.

And to tell you the truth I'd rather listen to Rolf Harris sing this as he's got more talent than Baddiel and Skinner. The only good thing I can say about them and Ian Brodie is that I like them being shorter than me.

You can't even compare this to 'Vindaloo' and if it reaches Number One I'll wipe my bum with razor blades for a month. Hopefully I'll never have to hear this crap again after the World Cup.

MEAT PIE, SAUSAGE ROLL – GRANDAD ROBERTS AND HIS SON ELVIS

One spin of this convinced me I would never let Grandad Roberts babysit for me. It sounds like me and my dad singing. The lyrics remind me of my mother's cooking skills at teatime when we were kids. It just needs those extra delicate lyrics, like chips and egg.

DON'T COME HOME TOO SOON – DEL AMITRI

I hope Scotland can play better football than the stuff Del Amitri, who I happen to love, have produced. The beginning sounds like Noel and Liam Gallagher high on eating potted paste butties for inspiration.

Basically, they would have been better off going down the railway station and getting every Scotsman drunk on Special Brew to sing a song.

TOP OF THE WORLD (OLE, OLE, OLE) – CHUMBAWUMBA

It sounds like Mary Hopkins with love eggs and it's a total waste of time.

We all go around saying what a pile of shit Chumbawumba are and how much we hate them, but

> they go around making damn good fucking beer-swilling, shagging, brainless moron music for the likes of me – until now. As a football song it isn't worth a toss, and even the leftie popsters will cringe when they hear it.

The article was accompanied by photos of Shaun in his yellow Ted Smith coat, holding CDs and making facial expressions to add emphasis to his literary tirade. The *Sport* were delighted with the piece, and the slightly psychotic Smithy suggested that Ryder should be asked to write a weekly column for the paper. Editor Livesey loved the idea.

TONY LIVESEY: I think the first move was made by Smithy. He suggested it. Smithy said he knew Shaun of old from when he used to do the Manchester DJ circuit, but he used to bullshit so I didn't believe him. But he suggested to me having Shaun as a columnist so I took the ball and ran with it. I just said to Shaun, 'You've got a full page in the paper to write what you want, as long as it's readable.'

SHAUN: It was actually me who spoke to Livesey about doing a regular column. Because I'd already done the single reviews with that kid Smithy I thought it would be alright to work with him. Obviously I was wrong.

Livesey struck a deal with Shaun and told Smithy to ghost-write the new weekly column with him. Being slightly dyslexic, Shaun would dictate the column to Smithy and the hack would knock it into shape.

A meeting was arranged at *Sport* HQ where Shaun stipulated one condition and a name was agreed upon. The column was to be called 'It's Great Talking Straight' – an obvious but effective pun on the title of the first Black Grape LP, *It's Great When You're Straight . . . Yeah!*

TONY LIVESEY: I gave Smithy the job of working with Shaun, which almost proved fatal later, and Shaun came in to see us. He had one demand about the column, which was that everyone who featured in it would be identified by their height rather than their age. Well, obviously, I was very impressed with this. I thought it was a gimmick this height thing, but he rattled off the height of every player in the England football squad. He knew them all off by heart. And we had a picture taken of him in the office and he insisted on standing on a chair, so he was majorly obsessed with height.

We had some press cards made up for him with his picture on and the *Sport* logo, which he would hand out to people. I thought the whole thing was brilliant. There's a real mystique about journalism that you get all these young thrusters at 22, who swan around in their sharp suits and get into places. I think it's great that we gave one of the biggest drug-addled brains in Britain access to practically anything he wanted, representing Her Majesty's press. It's a very typical *Sport* thing to do.

I told David [Sullivan – owner of Sport Newspapers] that we'd got Shaun Ryder and I don't think he'd heard of him because he said, 'Right, great.' But he'd obviously been asking around because a week later he rang back and said: 'That's absolutely brilliant that you've got Shaun Ryder, he's an icon for a generation.' So I think he'd been asking people what they thought and people had said he's the man for the *Sport*.

SMITHY: I thought the whole idea was fucking mega. I reckoned Shaun Ryder was probably the funniest bloke I'd ever met and the material he could give me to knock up for his column was hilarious, and everyone agreed. At the time I felt a bit sorry for the bloke, who was trying to piece his life back together after years on the smack. I thought the column would give the paper thousands of extra sales – it was a marriage made in heaven.

When we started working together, Ryder was being chaperoned virtually 24 hours a day for his own good by Too-Nice Tom, who was all too aware of the temptations for a man withdrawing from heroin addiction, and particularly a man with the narcotic appetite of Ryder. But Tom trusted me to look after him for one or two nights a week. Shaun would come down to my house and we would sit, play tunes and get pissed, get stoned and write the weekly column. It was a little bizarre at first.

The first time Shaun came round he got out of the car and puked over the next door neighbour's fence, which slightly perturbed the old dear living there, who was mowing her lawn at the time. I had a feeling then that it was going to be a bit of a rollercoaster ride.

Shaun's first column proper appeared in the *Sport* in the first week of July 1998 and was fairly serious in tone. It kicked off with a tirade against the alcohol and tobacco industry, and put forward the case for legalising soft drugs. From then on, the column changed dramatically from week to week. No two weeks were the same. Even if Shaun promised to tell you something in next week's amazing column, the reader could safely assume he'd have forgotten to do so by the time it came around.

As well as Shaun's take on the week's current events, there were spoof articles. The only staple element of his page – usually Page 9 – was the Celebrity Tits Out Spot, where he challenged famous ladies and sexual icons to doff their tops in the name of fun. Subjects/victims featured in this category have included everyone from Radio One's Jo Whiley to the Cadbury's Caramel Bunny Rabbit.

As the weeks rolled on, Shaun and Smithy were knocking out great columns and Ryder's mailbag at the *Sport* was bursting, even if it was with pictures of transsexuals for the first couple of weeks. Not that there's anything wrong with that, brothers and sisters; it's just a bit peculiar to see pictures of all those bits on the same person at the same time, that's all.

SMITHY: He was a paranoid bastard. He used to hate opening his own mail because he thought someone was going to send him razor blades through the post. All in all it was going well, though. We were even socialising together, and one day we decided to take our kids on a day out to an amusement park with Shaun's mate G-man and his daughter.

It all went a bit pear-shaped, though. As soon as we got into the place and the kids started eyeing up the various rides, Shaun decided he had to find the bar. But knowing him as I did, I knew he wouldn't be nipping in for a quick half. I was right. A female friend of Shaun's was with us and she ended up looking after the girls for the day because we finished up absolutely shit-faced.

Two hours later, the kiddies decided they wanted to see their dads, so Ryder, G-man and Smithy were dragged away from the bar by the girls and taken to watch a medieval-style pantomime. The kids loved it, but it was all too obvious that Ryder was a little worse for wear.

SMITHY: I could have died laughing. For some bizarre reason, Shaun had lesbians on his mind, and he decided to heckle the poor bastards who were dressed up in medieval suits of armour trying to entertain all the families.

So every time a new face appeared on the stage, he was shouting, 'Oi! Fat fucker! I bet your wife's a fucking lesbian! No, I bet *you're* a lesbian! And I bet your fucking horse is gay as well!' Not surprisingly, we were all asked to leave the show and I breathed a small sigh of relief, particularly as my five-year-old daughter was asking me what a 'fucking rug-munching lesbian' meant.

But that was just the start of the afternoon's hilarity as far as Shaun was concerned. We sauntered over to the fairground stalls, where Shaun's daughter Jael fancied a go at the hook-a-duck stall, with the promise of a big teddy bear as a prize. Little Jael failed to win the teddy bear, and Shaun was none-too-pleased that the spotty youth behind the stall refused to hand over the teddy bear anyway.

I remember that Shaun was very insistent that Jael should get a prize and the debate was getting a little heated. After about a minute, Shaun got sick of the conversation, so he leaped over the stall, grabbed a teddy bear and gave a menacing growl to the kid behind the counter, who obviously shat himself.

The kid must have radioed for help and pretty soon security guards were all over us like a dose of crabs. But instead of chucking us out, they recognised Shaun and let him off with giving his autograph. I bet that's not the first time that happened.

Shaun really didn't give a fuck. He gave the teddy to his kid and we all went back to the bar.

Ryder's relationship with Smithy, a man whose bald head has, in the past, caused him to be compared to a talking egg, was to take an absurd turn that very evening. Back at Smithy's house, Shaun revealed his big plan – for the pair of them to fuck off to Ibiza for a few days as guests of the Radio One roadshow, with the *Sport* picking up the bill.

Shaun had been invited to Ibiza by Radio One, who were staging a week of live broadcasts from the 'party capital of the world'. The plan was for him to visit a few clubs and review them for Steve Lamacq's show, *Lamacq Live*. Briggy Smale, from the Entertainment News department of the station, was to chaperone him around the island and the clubs and then interview him for the features.

Initially Smithy, who had by now been dubbed 'Mr Potato Head' by Shaun, thought that this was a terrifyingly bad idea. He knew he wouldn't be able to convince his gaffer Livesey to part with a wad of dosh merely for them to whoop it up in the sun, no matter how happy the editor was with the newspaper column.

However Ryder, as persuasive as ever, pointed out that there would be a bucketful of celebrity stories for Mr Potato Head to send to the paper when they arrived in Ibiza and Shaun hooked up with his showbiz mates. He also told Mr Potato Head that he would get to DJ at all the top nightclubs on the island. Mr Potato Head still occasionally worked as DJ Tintin, and was suddenly completely and utterly sold on the idea.

So the next day Mr Potato Head tackled Livesey, who reluctantly agreed on the condition that the duo would get value for money from the trip by unearthing great tabloid exposés on the stars. This decision by Livesey was possibly the greatest misjudgement in the history of British journalism.

TONY LIVESEY: Shaun's first few columns for the *Sport* had been quite readable, so we got a bit over-ambitious and the idea came up that there was this big Radio One party in Ibiza. Smithy said how about us going out and covering it, which sounded fantastic, because Shaun had been invited and would have access to all these people.

The tickets were booked. But the day before the trip, Mr Potato Head was summoned to a special news conference in the *Sport's* Ancoats HQ to discuss the task at hand. It became clear to him that Tony Livesey had very ambitious – and specific – requirements for the trip.

MR POTATO HEAD: It was quite simple. Tony was under the impression that we would be staying with the Radio One disc jockeys at their villa, and he wanted a picture of Zoë Ball at the poolside with her tits out. He was quite adamant about that. I was told to sneak a camera into all the top celebrity parties we went to and get a whole host of stories.

He suggested that once I'd taken the pics of Zoë with her tits out and various celebrities in states of alcohol- and drug-fuelled undress, I should lob the films over a garden wall where somebody would be waiting to send the pics back over to England.

I felt that this was quite a tall order, but Tony's last words to me that afternoon were, 'If you don't manage it, you're fucking sacked, you moron.' I was starting to have a very bad feeling about the trip. Getting these stories and pictures and trying to stop Shaun going mental in the party capital of the world was going to be one hell of a mindfuck.

It was fair to say that Mr Potato Head had his work cut out for him. He was clearly wary of his newly assigned role as chaperone to one of the world's naughtiest lads, and so prepared nervously to head off into the Balearics. Unfortunately for Mr Potato Head, Shaun had a very different agenda. He was going to forget all about the worthy strictures of life at Too-Nice Tom's and the miseries of heroin withdrawal and have one hell of a party.

After a small pre-departure hiccup, when Shaun couldn't find his passport and threatened to use his brother's (thankfully, he found his in the nick of time), the pair headed off for Leeds/Bradford airport. There, Shaun had some words of advice for Mr Potato Head:

MR POTATO HEAD: He told me not to drink on the plane. He said that he was bang in the middle of the public eye on that plane and he didn't want anybody to see either himself or anybody with him get arseholed. I bowed to his superior knowledge of these situations and agreed.

So there I was drinking fucking mineral water on the flight and he was sat in the aisle seat behind me, presumably, I thought, doing the same. But just before we were about to land, I stood up and looked over to the seat behind me. Shaun had about 100 empty miniature vodka bottles scattered all over him and was talking to the middle-aged woman next to him about oral sex with a huge fucking grin on his face. This was the start of the mother of all benders.

TONY LIVESEY: Yeah, we packed them off and it appears they were arguing like brother and sister from the minute they got on the plane. Shaun insisted that Smithy didn't drink because he was now a journalist doing a job, and then sat behind him on the plane and got pissed the whole trip. When they landed in Ibiza he was absolutely wrecked, and it just went from bad to worse.

The plane touched down and the pair were to be met at Ibiza airport by Briggy Smale.

BRIGGY SMALE: Basically Shaun was going to come over, we'd go to a couple of clubs and I'd talk to him afterwards, and use that as a review of what was going on out in Ibiza. The idea was if you're going to go and experience Ibiza, you want to hear from the person who's going to get the most out of it, and then more, and totally create their own madness. So Shaun was perfect. Strange things happen to Shaun. They find him.

But as Shaun and Potato Head wheeled their luggage, Ryder's duty-free and Smithy's box of records into the arrivals lounge, the hack's face turned as white as a sheet. Briggy wasn't alone. With her was a big guy named Huey, who was working as a cameraman for the Radio One website. Huey was also a DJ, from Manchester.

'Oh shit!' screamed Mr Potato Head.

'You fucking cunt!' shouted Huey.

It transpired that the *Sport*'s very own answer to Smashy, that is DJ Tintin aka Mr Potato Head, had nicked a box of Huey's records while they were DJing together almost seven years earlier. The scrawny

Potato Head had been avoiding the muscle-bound Huey ever since.

BRIGGY SMALE: As soon as Shaun and Smithy had walked out at the airport, the camera guy I was with said, 'Oh my God, that bald one nicked my records years ago.' I was like, 'Oh dear.'

Naturally, Shaun saw the funny side and proceeded to laugh his bollocks off, much to the confusion of Smithy, who didn't know whether to join in the laughter, or brace himself to have his face rearranged. Thankfully, and quite amazingly, Huey was in a forgiving mood.

So the foursome sped into the centre of Ibiza with a bottle of vodka, some narcotics (but the author has to point out that the Radio One employee was NOT joining in that side of things) and a set of porno playing cards. These had been bought by Briggy as a present for Shaun to keep him amused on the drive into San Antonio.

BRIGGY SMALE: I remember when Shaun arrived I was nervous about looking after him. I'd met him on a couple of occasions before that, but never had the chance to spend much time with him. I knew he was a real lad and I was just hoping he wasn't on a mad one because he was my responsibility for the night.

I know we were in Ibiza, but I had my sensible work head on, so I got to the airport and was thinking, 'Oh my God what's going to happen?', and he came out of the arrivals gate and recognised me immediately. He's got that kind of memory where he can't remember how old he is but he can remember someone he had a chat with for a few seconds fifteen years ago.

So he went, 'All right B,' and I said, 'Oh, all right, yeah!' Then he said 'I want a quiet one this time, B.' And I was thinking, 'Oh good, it isn't going to be too messy.' Whereas, in actual fact, it did get very, very messy.

I even managed to shut him up for a while, because I'd decided to buy him a present to break the ice. There's a shop down in San Antonio which sells porno playing cards, and I got him this pack which were really revolting. I gave them to him and he was flabbergasted because they were really disgusting.

MR POTATO HEAD: Shaun was particularly impressed with the Jack of Clubs, which featured a leggy blonde having an orgasm whilst sat on a banana.

After driving around for two hours unsuccessfully trying to locate Annie Nightingale's villa – Shaun particularly wanted to hook up with her, even though she was undoubtedly asleep – they found a bar that was still serving booze at 6 a.m. and continued the session.

BRIGGY SMALE: Shaun mentioned during the course of the evening that things weren't good with his marriage and that some manager or other was trying to sue him for money, but he didn't seem to be letting it get him down. Everything was OK – until Smithy got going.

Indeed, while Ryder was already whooping it up with a bevy of 18–30 holiday girls, his *Sport* escort Mr Potato Head had other things on his mind. His editor's words were still ringing round his head.

So Smithy, the ultimate professional, took Shaun to one side to discuss the ins-and-outs of grabbing some snatch pictures of the stars. Unfortunately for them, Briggy overheard the conversation.

BRIGGY SMALE: I knew somebody was coming with Shaun, but I had no idea *what* was coming. Basically I knew Shaun wrote for the *Sport*, but I didn't realise what sort of person Smithy was.

They were pretty quiet for the first half hour or so, but then Shaun went up to some guy and asked, 'Where's the prozzies, mate?' I was just praying it didn't all come back on me.

Then, over the course of the next couple of hours, this Smithy guy started saying things like, 'Can you get us into the Radio One DJs' villas?' And I was saying, 'Well, no, I can't even get in there myself, and I wouldn't do even if I could.'

I was trying to get Shaun to see Annie Nightingale, and I'd get Shaun into the clubs and that was it, but this Smithy man was obviously very stupid because he didn't realise I was connected with Radio One and therefore would protect the people who were there. And he started saying: 'I want to get into the villas. I've got a camera, and I've got a lad who's coming over to take pictures and I'm going to get pictures of the female DJs' tits.' So, of course, I was saying, 'Oh no you're not!' I think he wanted pictures of Zoë and Jo, they would have been just great for him. I said to Shaun, 'That's not right, Shaun, obviously I can't do that. It's not what we talked about.'

Then we stopped at this English bar in San Antonio and Smithy was still banging on about taking these pictures. I was getting really uncomfortable, because I didn't want it to hinder what Shaun and I were going to do with the Roadshow. And I didn't want to spend any more time in his company, because I could have got sacked if Radio One thought I had anything to do with whatever he got up to.

Then Smithy was trying to take pictures of my jugs while I was sat on Shaun's knee, and Shaun was offering me £200 to, er, get my baps out. He was saying, 'Whap your baps out, B, they're gorgeous.' But I'm sorry, I don't do that.

The whole thing was so silly. Shaun was telling Smithy, 'She works for Radio One, don't tell her that, don't tell her you're trying to sneak photos of DJs' tits.' And Smithy was going, 'Yeah, so what I've got is this lad sitting in a tree and I'm going to chuck him a camera and he's going to get pictures of all their tits and we'll put it on the front page.' Smithy was going on and on, and Shaun could see I was getting really unhappy because it had got to the point where I was thinking, Right, I'm going to have to ditch Shaun as well now, because if they're part of the same thing, and I'm having the wool pulled over my eyes, then there's nothing else I can do. So I said to Shaun that I was unhappy about the whole situation. I said, 'I really want to work with you, but this guy's really freaking me out.'

So then Shaun started shouting at Smithy and calling him Potato Head. Smithy couldn't understand this, because he had a deadline and needed pictures of famous people's tits. Things were getting heated and Smithy couldn't realise the more he said these things he wanted the more edgy I got and the more Shaun was getting annoyed too. Smithy kept saying he had this guy apparently hiding in the trees, but when you looked at him all he had was one of those disposable cameras like you get in Boots. It's hadn't even got a long lens – it was just this crappy disposable camera. I said I couldn't go on with this, and would have to take them back to their hotel. Smithy said, 'Fine, take me back,' and then for one reason or another, whether it was because he'd had enough, or because he wanted to help me out, Shaun snapped and kicked Smithy right out of the car.

Nobody knew where we were. We were just on this dirt track, miles from anywhere. Smithy had no mobile and no idea where he was staying. Picture it. It was about four in the morning, and this guy stood there by a dirt track, with nothing but pitch black, no traffic, not even a street light and about half a mile from a main road. He could have been in any country, anywhere in the world and he wouldn't have known. And to this day I have absolutely no idea what happened to him and how he got back from there. But I do know that on his return he said something like, 'Shaun poked me in the eye, Shaun told me to fuck off, Shaun was really horrible.'

I think Ibiza was a bonding experience for me and Shaun because we were both with this complete idiot, and so we had someone to poke fun at. There's nothing starry about Shaun, nothing at all. Oh, and apparently I look like a policewoman.

Shaun insists that it was Smithy who let slip his foul plans to the Radio One announcer. Smithy insists that it was the intoxicated Shaun who tactlessly revealed Smithy's tabloid tactics. Perhaps we shall never know the truth about that one. However, this *fracas* definitely marked the beginning of the end for the gruesome twosome's working and personal relationship.

Two hours later, Shaun and Mr Potato Head were both back at their ridiculously overpriced hideaway holiday apartment. Smithy tried to tell Shaun that he should stop boozing and get some sleep, but when he turned his back, Shaun slipped away and legged it back into town for some dawn debauchery. Mr Potato Head wouldn't see him again for eighteen hours.

Smithy became more and more worried about his partner's absence until finally, with the journalist-cum-DJ starting to freak out big time over the imminent prospect of life on the dole, Shaun returned. With a buxom beauty in tow.

'Where the fuck have you been, you daft twat?' exclaimed Smithy, who now had just 30 minutes to somehow get a story of some kind telephoned over to the *Daily Sport*. But Shaun couldn't answer. He was off his head. And in a very, very bad way.

MR POTATO HEAD: I'd seen him off it plenty of times before, but this time was different. I was worried that he'd done the very thing that Tom Bruggen trusted me not to let him do – gone back on the gear.

So Smithy scooped Ryder up, and tried to revive his flagging pal by taking him for breakfast at a local beachside restaurant. But he could get no sense from Shaun, who at this point was having trouble forming any other word than 'fuck'. Smithy knew he had to face the music. So he went to a nearby telephone booth and dialled Manchester to give the paper a progress report. The call was picked up at the other end by Paul Carter, the paper's news editor.

'So where's your copy, then?' enquired Carter.

'Erm, I'm just trying to cobble something together now. I've had a difficult time trying to locate Shaun,' came the weary reply.

'So where is Shaun now?' asked Carter.

Smithy was virtually braindead from his night on the town, as well as weary from eighteen anxious hours of seeing his job disappear. Still, he was a professional doing a job. The job was to report back to England the goings-on in Ibiza as he experienced them with Shaun Ryder (as well as getting a picture of Zoë Ball's tits). So when Carter asked him where Shaun was, it was all Smithy could do to answer it as honestly as he could.

He looked over his shoulder to check, before inform-ing Carter that their star columnist was currently, '. . . face down in a bowl of soup.'

To this day, Carter maintains that that was probably the funniest line he's ever heard. Smithy quickly knocked up a 'It's Great Talking Straight In Ibiza' column on his laptop, fired it down the phoneline, and walked back over to rescue Shaun from his chicken soup.

'If it weren't for his peaked baseball cap, he would have drowned in it completely,' recalls Smithy. What a way to go.

After a good sleep, Ryder woke up refreshed and the pair headed into town for some serious partying. Smithy knew he wouldn't have to send any more copy over to the *Sport* for another 24 hours, and it was finally arranged for him to DJ the next night at the infamous Cafe Mambo. Shaun insisted that he played 'One Nation Under A Groove' by Funkadelic at least three times, but DJ Tintin/Talking Egg/Mr Potato Head felt he could live with that.

So the pair, feeling a lot more relaxed, started some serious partying. After visiting the Radio One Road-show, drinking with Norman Cook, aka Fatboy Slim, and necking a quantity of drugs which Keith Richards would quake in his pixie boots at, Shaun was asked for a quick interview by Sky TV. Perhaps it wasn't the best time for him to face the world, but Ryder has plenty of experience of being interviewed whilst completely out of his skull.

'Let me tell you why I'm here in Ibiza,' he en-lightened the interviewer. 'I'm clubbing for the *Sport*, writing for the *Sport*, drinking for the *Sport*, eating for the *Sport* and taking drugs for the *Sport*.' He and Smithy continued to party the night – and morning – away in a hideous state of excess. However, things were to take a turn for the worse when Shaun decided, at 6 a.m., that he wanted to visit a brothel.

MR POTATO HEAD: It completely freaked me out. We were so off it that I could barely see two feet in front of me, but Shaun wanted me to get in the car and drive him around in search of a blow job. We had an almighty row, which ended up with us throwing each other over the bonnet of the hire car, but Shaun won the day. So there we were, driving all around the fucking island with the dawn breaking searching for a fucking brothel. I remember thinking the day after that I wasn't even sure what side of the road I was driving on.

We didn't get to find a brothel and I was extremely glad. Because I knew that the state Shaun was in, if he went into a brothel he wouldn't have come out for another three days and he would have literally spunked all of his money.

The pair eventually arrived back at their apartment and the Colombian marching powder was chopped out on the table. But Potato Head, not a person usually known for saying no to refreshments of the gum-numbing variety, just couldn't face nipping into Shaun's bedroom for a refresher.

MR POTATO HEAD: It was his feet. The unbelievable smell of his feet is legendary. The pong was so bad that I went outside and puked off the balcony.

There was to be no respite, though, for Potato Head. He gratefully fell asleep, but once again Ryder was on party overload and slipped away. When the hack crawled out of his pit just three hours later and realised Ryder was missing again, he went berserk.

It was time to write another column for the *Sport* and Ryder was once again AWOL, location unknown. This time, Smithy was a little more candid with the staff back at the *Sport*.

'Get us the fuck out of here,' he begged news editor Carter. 'Ryder's on a fucking drink and drugs suicide mission and I think I'm having a fucking nervous breakdown.'

The deadly duo's stay in Ibiza was supposed to last four days, but Smithy was convinced the only policy was to get the hell out of there. Carter miraculously arranged for new flight tickets to bring them back to Manchester via Barcelona the next day. Shaun, meanwhile, was still nowhere to be seen. Smithy conducted a frantic search around the clubs and bars of San Antonio together with a *Sport* photographer called Benji, who had been told to hook up with Smithy after getting a boat from Majorca where he was on another job.

MR POTATO HEAD: That was all I needed. If it wasn't bad enough trying to locate Shaun I had to put up with Benji, who hadn't slept for 48 hours. The poor bastard was so fucking tired that he was ranting and literally foaming at the mouth. He eventually fell asleep in the car and I just left him there for four hours before he buggered off back to Majorca without a single picture of Shaun to take back with him.

Smithy himself was due to appear that night as DJ Tintin at Cafe Mambo. What the hell, he figured. He might as well do the gig and get some kind of satisfaction from the trip. So he hit the turntables at the beachside club, and as soon as he slipped 'One Nation Under A Groove' on to the decks, who miraculously appeared in the bar like, well, the shopkeeper from *Mr Benn*? You guessed it. That man Ryder.

By now though DJ Tintin, aka Mr Potato Head, was way beyond arguing the point that Ryder had forgotten his responsibilities to the *Sport*. He came out from behind the decks, and after he told Shaun that they were both flying home at 6 a.m. the following morning – by now just eight hours away – they decided that a last blow-out was on the agenda.

Shaun and Smithy settled their differences and headed, with a crew of Manchester exiles, to the Manumission club. They ended up drinking champagne backstage with the sexy bunny girl waitresses and a transvestite dancer called Fifi. And then the shit *really* hit the fan.

When Mr Potato Head asked Shaun to leave with him for the airport, Shaun decided to turn nasty with the hapless hack, accusing him of being a party pooper and ruining his trip. An outraged Smithy was having none of it. Bottles of champagne were thrown, tables were overturned, and the fighting odd couple finally had to be pulled apart.

Shaun insisted that he was staying on Ibiza with his new pals. A despairing Potato Head tried to reason with him but eventually gave up the ghost and handed him the original plane ticket. He merely prayed that Ryder's pals could look after him for the rest of the week, and make sure he made it to the airport for his flight the following Sunday.

MR POTATO HEAD: I did my best to try and get him to the airport, but in the end I just thought 'Fuck him'. I'd had more than enough of him and all the fucking shit I had to put up with. When we took his bags out of the car we were both ready to lamp one another. From that point on we washed our hands of each other.

Knackered, Smithy drove to the airport and flew out of the whole mess. When he touched down in Manchester, he went home to take some heavy sedatives for his nerves and vowed never to work with Shaun Ryder again.

MR POTATO HEAD: It all got so fucked up in Ibiza, but I still think Shaun is a great character and a great talent and I've still got a lot of respect for him. I remember when he finally came back from Ibiza and I told him that I wouldn't be doing the column any more, I wished him the best of luck with it. But at the time, back in San Antonio, I felt like killing the bastard and burying him in a shallow grave.

Still, I'm not one to bear grudges. If I bumped into him in town I'd happily have a pint with him. But only if he was fucking buying.

TONY LIVESEY: I think Smithy panicked, because he's basically a sports hack and he's got no experience of handling a columnist or a major breaking news story. So when Shaun was going face-first in his soup every dinnertime, and I'd said to Smithy I want loads of stories every day with pictures or you're sacked, he panicked.

So we were getting calls back here saying Shaun had vanished. Apparently they had a fist fight, Shaun got hooked up with some local druggies, was drinking until 6 a.m., didn't do any work at all, and the worst thing of all was that we'd paid for all the tickets and everything. Then Shaun didn't come back. It was an absolute nightmare.

Smithy came back on his own, vowing never to work with Shaun again. I had handbags at dawn with Smithy over that, and then we had to find Shaun again. I must admit I felt a sense of responsibility for him. I knew the state he was in, and I thought any day now we're going to get the call, or it will be in the *Sun* that he's dead.

Shaun Ryder didn't die out in Ibiza. However, he did take off on an epic bender that was to see him spend another three weeks on the island.

BRIGGY SMALE: Shaun actually rang me one afternoon, about 3.30 p.m., and said, 'All right B, do you know where I am?' I said, 'No, where are you?' and he said, 'No, do *you* know where I am? Because I don't.'

Then later that same evening, some people rang me up and asked me to go to Mambo to look after him because he had my phone number in his pocket. So I went down and he wasn't there, but someone said: 'You should see the size of the lovebite on Shaun Ryder's wife's neck.' I told them his wife wasn't in Ibiza.

Radio One DJ Chris Moyles also met Shaun one day in Mambo, which was becoming his regular haunt.

CHRIS MOYLES: I saw Shaun in Mambo, and he was OK. He was all [best Manc accent] 'How's your mum, how's your dad, how's Comedy Dave? Is Dave here? Mega brilliant.' So I invited him to Manumission that evening and sorted him out for tickets.

Then I met him in the VIP room at Manumission later on and he was . . . bollocksed is a nice way of putting it. I was asking him if he was alright and he was fucking wobbling all over the place and had a woman with him. So he turned to the woman and by way of introduction, said, 'This is Dave Pearce.'

And I was like, 'No, it's Chris, nice to meet you.' But Shaun was insistent, and kept asking, 'Are you alright, Dave?'

'No, it's Chris.'

And he went, 'Yeah, Chris Moyles,' and then I . . . had to go.

It was at that same Manumission party that a picture of Shaun was taken that made it into the pages of a UK music magazine. The photograph showed him kipping on a couch in the middle of the full-on raging party at

Manumission. Some well-wishers had spotted the prowling paparazzi and tried to get Shaun well inside the VIP area before the inevitable picture was taken. They were too late. By the time Briggy and some others spotted him the snapper had escaped and sent his image along a telephone line back to London.

BRIGGY SMALE: I only saw Shaun one more time in Ibiza and that was in Manumission where the snappers got that picture of him asleep. Shaun was sleeping, dribbling, on a sofa in what is supposed to be the biggest, loudest, best club in the world, the sauciest nightspot in Ibiza.

I did my best to keep the photographers away from him, because for all the things that people think about Shaun, he's a really decent guy and I see him as a bit of a genius, so I've got huge respect for him. And the least I could do was get him out of the view of the snappers, because they were all trying to make out he was still on the gear and stuff. I felt very sure that he was very pissed and probably stoned and nothing else.

So I thought if people see a picture of him like *that*, you know what the headlines are going to be and he doesn't deserve that. So we tried to move him because unfortunately he was right by the VIP entrance so they could photograph him. It took four people to usher him down there and he carried on sleeping for a good few hours.

TONY LIVESEY: It's now legendary this trip that Shaun went on in Ibiza. You hear that he was buying drugs off anyone who would give him drugs, selling his shoes, all that sort of stuff. And I think people just used him as a party turn out there. They got him wasted so that he'd perform for them. I don't mean sing for them – they just wanted the Shaun Ryder antics.

The next person who bumped into Shaun during his Missing In Action tour of Ibiza was DJ Norman Cook, aka Fatboy Slim. Norman, who met his future wife Zoë Ball during the same week (it's not on record whether he photographed her tits), was playing at one of the island's clubs when he spotted Shaun coming over to him in a bar.

The DJ was understandably apprehensive. Years earlier, as the bass player in indie band the Housemartins, Norman had played on the same bill as Happy Mondays at a gig at Dingwalls, in London. The experience had left him scarred for life. The Mondays entourage had terrified the Housemartins, who barricaded their dressing room door until the Mondays went on for their set, at which point they'd legged it from the venue.

However, when Shaun and Fatboy were reunited that warm Ibiza night, they got on famously.

FATBOY SLIM: We had an amazing conversation about absolute bollocks. It was in Bar M, after a particularly long weekend, on the Sunday night. I'd been playing Manumission and I was going on to do this thing on Radio One. To be honest I've always been quite scared of Shaun because of his reputation. And when he came towards me in Ibiza I thought, Oh my God, he probably thinks I'm some southern poof or something.

But he just said, 'Hey, Norman, can I have my photo taken with you?' And I was really chuffed. Until then I'd kind of figured I was the sort of person he wouldn't really like.

I've met him once or twice since and every time we've both been very . . . excitable. We don't sit and talk about business. I seem to remember having a bet with him about whether my PA would show his girlfriend his ginger pubes in return for her showing him her false teeth. It's always that kind of conversation.

He does give off this aura of . . . you know . . . *being Shaun Ryder*.

Meanwhile, the concerned *Daily Sport* were still desperate to recover their errant columnist. However, the only contact number they had was for his regular bar, Cafe Mambo, where the person on the other end of the line spoke fluent Spanish, German and French, but not a word of English.

There were frequent heated discussions between a hapless hack on one end and an increasingly pissed off cafe manager on the other.

The *Sport* even went to the lengths of designing spaghetti-western-style 'Wanted' posters and sending somebody out to post them the length and breadth of the island.

TONY LIVESEY: Yeah, we printed 'Wanted' posters that we sent out to Ibiza to try to find him. We also put them in the paper and put in a phoneline asking people if they'd seen him because we needed to find him.

Then, eventually, somebody rang us to say they'd got hold of him and we paid that guy money to get Shaun back to the airport. We never heard one word from Shaun while he was in Ibiza. We didn't have his columns at all for two weeks while he was out there.

Shaun Ryder eventually touched down back in the UK three weeks after he'd gone out to Ibiza for four days. It transpired that during his lengthy overstay he'd shacked up with a couple of girls who had let him crash at their San Antonio pad and who took him partying every night. There are worse ways of spending your time.

TONY LIVESEY: I think at that point any sane editor would have sacked him, but I just had this feeling that he was going to come good.

Before going to Ibiza Shaun had moved out of Too-Nice Tom's. Tom's wife was nearing the nine-month mark of her pregnancy, and Tom was worried because Shaun had been seen hanging around with some known junkies. Through a pal he had arranged a place for Shaun to stay.

Shaun's living situation now was very different. His Ibiza bender was over with, but he was no longer the clean-living lodger trying to smarten up his act, he was home alone after all the traumatic and painful detox work, and in danger of getting bored. And we all know what happens when Shaun gets bored.

TOO-NICE TOM: As Shaun moved out, I told him, 'I'll always love you, you twisted fucked-up maniac.'

Tony Livesey still wanted Shaun to write his *Sport* column, but after the harrowing Ibiza experience, the shellshocked Mr Potato Head wanted nothing to do with the singer. So the job, or the poisoned chalice, as Smithy was insisting on calling it, was handed over to a reporter called Lorne Jackson.

This short-lived plan was an unmitigated disaster. Jackson is a fine reporter, but speaks with such a heavy Glaswegian accent that even fellow Glaswegians have trouble understanding him. Shaun's Salford tones can also be hard to follow. Nevertheless, *Sport* features editor Sarah Stephens shut the pair in a room together to come up with a column. She was forced to admit defeat after it became clear that neither could tell what the fuck the other was saying.

Which is where this book's author comes in. I'd only been a writer at the *Sport* for eight months when I was assigned Shaun's column. I wasn't that keen at the time. Spending one night a week of my own time with him, plus having to write the column up afterwards, seemed a real pain in the arse. It soon blossomed, though, into a wonderful excuse to get loaded with one of the funniest people I've ever met.

My first meeting with Shaun was at a steakhouse in Burnley. He had just moved out of Too-Nice Tom's into a rented gaff nearby in Carlton Road. The steakhouse was no VIP gaff, just a run-of-the-mill family-oriented restaurant with a smell of wax polish and Lambert and Butler. The decor was mass-produced Olde Worlde, with the chain's logo-strewn carpet lit by hanging lights over wooden tables. Situated next to Burnley's only cinema, it even had a play area for kids.

If the staff seemed cautious of Shaun as he ordered his favourite dish, a plate of ribs with no sauce, it was with good reason. I found out later that this was because the night before he thought someone had spat in his food, so he'd offered to carry out unsterilised surgery on the waiter's left eye with his cutlery. Away from Too-Nice Tom's care, Ryder had clearly been hitting a downward spiral.

Despite this, we hit it off and started producing some great *Sport* columns together. Some weeks I'd find Shaun on a roll and just sit back and lap it up, while others he'd be more lethargic and need prompting. He'd always come up with something, though, and the subject matter has to be the most diverse of any column on the planet, covering everything from the fashion sense of 70s cop duo Starsky and Hutch, to massage parlour reviews and the coolness of *Hong Kong Phooey*.

In fact, the review of local brothels was one of Shaun's most popular columns, and typical of the wit and wisdom of 'It's Great Talking Straight' with Shaun Ryder . . .

IT'S GREAT TALKING STRAIGHT

This week, geezers, I've been doing a very 'ARD job, touring ALL the massage parlours round Manchester, just so I can let you lucky bastards know which is the best.

Now let me tell you, dudes, Manchester Piccadilly Sauna, just over the road from my new offices at the *Sport* has come out tops.

It's got a big f***-off Olympic-sized swimming pool and absolutely every girl that works there is a qualified masseuse. They're also all ex-supermodels.

I'm going to open up an account there, dudes, because you're treated like a king, instead of wham, bam, f***ing tin of spam like some places. It's a full kung-fu massage, not rushed, not nasty, just . . .

I mean I tried a load of others, but they didn't even come close. Take the Wherethefukami massage parlour in Salford. The massage consisted of three headbutts, a kick in the bollocks and a stamp on the face. And there was no set price, they just took out of my pocket what I had in there.

Next one was in Burnley called Oomigubbins, where I was massaged by a blow-up doll, which turned out to be me grandma's sister's cousin.

If you've got a bit of dollar, then head for the Pretentious massage parlour in Worsley, which is the posh part of Salford. Guaranteed it's full of tight twats.

Snotty bastards go to the Prim and Proper, in piss-posh Hale. You get a real massage, body lotion, aromatherapy, reflexology – a waste of money.

In Old Trafford I visited the Stretford Big-Ender in the shadow of Manchester United's ground and close to Manchester Police HQ. Not nice. It's just full of cops, dentists and large packets of adult nappies.

The people in there weren't my cup of tea, they were quite wet. In fact it was full of big babies.

Oh, and stay away from the Fish and Vinegar Sauna in Pendlebury, you come out with unwanted pets.

The article caused absolute chaos for the Piccadilly Sauna, which is a *bona fide* sauna in Ancoats, Manchester, and doesn't have an Olympic-size swimming pool. They were deluged with clients who arrived with false expectations after reading it. But it didn't take a genius to figure out that Shaun was taking the piss. It's what he does best.

So over the summer of 1998 and beyond, I'd meet up with Shaun once every week to concoct his column. There was no doubt by now that Ryder and the *Sport* were soulmates. Here are a few more typical snippets . . .

TRAINS AT IT AGAIN

This f***ing saga with the trains is getting so bad I'm starting to take it personally. Last week I was coming back from London on the 8 p.m. train when there's this announcement that the engine supposed to be pulling the train is f***ed before we'd even left the station. So I'm in me seat waiting for the f***er to go when at 8.20 p.m. there's another announcement over the loudspeakers as someone who sounds like they're chewing a packet of cotton wool says they're having to bring another one down from Manchester to London. Anyway, I'm starving and I think, f*** this I'm off to get a burger. And I ask this bloke on the platform what time the train will be going. He says, 'Don't know mate. Haven't got a clue.'

Fine, I thought, I left my bags on the train and went to get one of those burgers you get from train stations which cost more than the third world f***ing debt, a paper and a Ribena. I'm five minutes and when I get back it's gone with my bags.

So I get right on the phone to G-man back in Manchester telling him to collect them from lost property at the station. Only as I put the phone down, I turn round to where I put my burger, my paper and my unopened Ribena ... and it's f***ing gone. There's this bloke putting it in his rubbish bin.

Basically the twat who told me he didn't know when it was going must have thought it was highly amusing because it f***ed off just three minutes later. Cheers, mate.

I finally got back about 2 a.m. And Manchester was like Dodge City. Have you ever tried reclaiming lost property from Manchester Piccadilly? Well, for a start, to ring up Manchester you first get put through to Glasgow. They put you through to somewhere else, they don't know what the f*** you're on about, and one number we got given was for some woman on Customer Services who told us: 'You shouldn't be ringing me on this number. How did you get this number?'

So big thanks to all at the train company who once again went out of their way to make sure my journey ran about as smoothly as the f***ing Pepsi-Max roller coaster.

WEATHER GIRLS
Where do the BBC get all these weather girls from? They know absolutely f***-all about weather apart from being constantly wet.

CAPRICE
Caprice is in the pop business now but she shot to fame as the bloody Wonderbra girl. What is the point of getting someone who doesn't need a Wonderbra to

advertise Wonderbras? She's got a right big pair of wongs.

WANKERS OF THE WEEK

The staff at the new Hugo Boss shop in Manchester. I went in there, spent £1,000 on jumpers and they wouldn't give me a penny on discount. The tossers.

ANIMAL HOSPITAL

No shit, guess who I saw out and about in Manchester's Gay Village this week . . . none other than that megastar Rolf Harris.

That's right the man famous for his didgeridoo and wobble board. He's also renowned for his song about 'Two Little Boys'.

Well, here he was with pals looking like he was having a great time. It turned out he was in Manchester for an episode of *Animal Hospital* where he rescues six hamsters left to die on a rubbish tip.

Like I say he looked like he was having a great time, old Rolf, but there was no sign of the hamsters. I can't imagine where they might have got to.

EMMERDALE

They always say owners start to look like their hounds. Well Emmerdale's Paddy Kirk, 3′2″ has started turning into Mandy Dingle.

Fat vet Paddy, 38-38-38, has been proper stitched up by his mum who's paying off Mandy – the reason widescreen telly was invented – loads of dosh NOT to marry him. That's fair enough, mums get really f***ing narked when you bring home a bird that's uglier than them, they want you to bring some f***ing supermodel home, not some bitch.

So who is Mandy marrying in this true-to-life account of life in the Yorkshire Dales? – er, her cousin . . . Nuff said.

ROBIN COOK

Well, f***ing hell, news of the week has to be that ugly bastard Robin Cook. His ex-missus has just bubbled him for allegedly shagging six birds behind her back, popping sleeping pills like Smarties, and falling asleep on the floor after downing a bottle of brandy.

Do you want a ***king job Rob? We're having a bit of trouble finding Bez at the moment, no one knows where the f*** he is.

But how does he do it? That's what every bloke in Britain is thinking right now. Has he got a giant knob, or has he got a tiny one and feels he has to put it about? Still it's good to hear that at least one of the Government likes ladies.

SWAMPY

There's a bit of a battle going on at the moment between eco-warriors and Manchester Airport over a proposed new runway. They first moved in about three years ago and started digging tunnels, living in trees and everything, and they sound like the new seven dwarves with daft names like Swampy, Grubby and Farty.

I'm behind these people who are doing their best to save the environment. In fact, I've thought about joining them. I'll go up there with a bottle of brandy and a spliff, call myself Toadstool and cement myself to a bulldozer. Then I can call myself an eco-warrior. That's a f***ing silly name, innit? People just think they are all dirty unwashed buggers. But if they had suits on, a side-parting and spoke like they had a plum in their mouth they'd get listened to. That's a sad testament to how we judge people by how they look and dress rather than what they do.

I mean Einstein was a right scruffy f***er, wasn't he? And Nelson Mandela, f***ing hell he's done more time than me! So good luck to anyone who's got the balls to make a stand.

Unsurprisingly, the *Sport*'s managing editor declared himself delighted with the sterling and opinionated efforts of his new star columnist.

TONY LIVESEY: I just want to stress how important the job is that Shaun's done on his column. It's so hard to find good big name columnists. In my opinion you only have to look at Johnny Vaughan in the *Sunday Mirror*. He's great on television but his column's shite. It really is tripe. You could argue we stumbled across Shaun, but he's brilliant.

If Shaun wasn't so outrageous I think he would have been poached by another paper. Shaun's very loyal to us, though, because with our paper there are no rules whatsoever. I just think he has this attitude to life which is basically 'Fuck everyone' and that's what we're about, really. In the nicest possible way we like to give the establishment the finger, and he seems to have been doing that for a long time.

The lowest point was when he jumped ship in Ibiza. When he jumped ship and chinned my sports editor and didn't come back. I was frantically ringing round all weekend trying to find him because I knew whatever happened I would end up picking up the bill. But we got over that, and now he's great.

I didn't know when I took him on that he'd be as funny as he is. I had this vague idea that he'd have all these rock anecdotes, and he'd trot out the day he did this with Bono or that with Keith Allen. But it's turned out ten times better than I thought it would because he's actually a funny guy; he's very original. People on the *News Of The World* envy us that column even though it's probably a bit too ripe for them. There's a columnist in the *Sun* now, a comedian called Mickey Hutton, and he's shit. If you toned down the language Shaun would wipe the floor with him. That's why it's stayed the pace. If Shaun was just a novelty act it would have all been over after six weeks.

Shaun actually replaced Bernard Manning in the *Sport*. Bernard had been with the paper for about ten years, but towards the end his jokes were generally recycled and we didn't feel he represented the modern cutting edge that we wanted. We'd been trying to modernise the *Daily Sport* for the last three or four years and Bernard didn't really fit any more.

When we sacked Bernard we didn't have Shaun in mind. But he's been a perfect replacement because he's humorous and he impresses our readers. Towards the end Bernard wasn't working out because, although we don't like to bow down to the PC brigade, they've generally done a job on Bernard and he's became *persona non grata* all over the bloody country. I think Bernard's like Benny Hill – retrospectively, he'll be remembered fondly.

I leave the drugs out of this. We don't promote drugs and I've never taken drugs, but otherwise Shaun seems to stand for everything we do, which is to say anything and be outrageous and controversial. Not many papers do that any more. And all the pop stars today are manufactured and have got nothing to say. They're not interesting people, whereas Shaun has some history. But I must admit, in the nicest possible way, he tries my patience to the limit.

But Shaun's done the job. He's come in, replaced Bernard, and been very, very funny.

Many music and celebrity figures found themselves both horrified and highly impressed with the cavalier disregard with which Shaun's new column flouted journalistic convention and social niceties.

CHRIS MOYLES: Shaun's got class, hasn't he? I read his column in the *Sport* once and he said he'd like to see Jo Whiley naked because, 'She's got a good rack on her,' or something like that. I just thought, Isn't that great? This modern music legend talking about Jo Whiley, this serious DJ who knows everything about music, and he just says, 'I bet she's got great tits.'

That just says it all to me, because you know it's true. There's probably some slight irony in there . . . but I wouldn't imagine there's very much.

STEVE LAMACQ: Profile-wise, the first time I noticed Shaun Ryder again after Black Grape was when he started writing for the *Sport* newspaper. I thought this was quite an incredible thing. I mean, you heard various bits and pieces about Shaun's gonna do this or that, or he wants to do something but he can't because there's litigation in the air, there's all these various problems, but then he turns up in the *Sport*, actually enjoying himself!

There are so many terrible, up-their-own-arse columnists in various newspapers. I think Shaun's life is probably loads more interesting than most. The only problem with Shaun is the likelihood that he'll libel loads of people and get himself and the paper sued. There must be so many stories that he can't tell for one reason or another. But as a Voice Of The People type, there are far worse writers in the world.

I've read his column a couple of times and it was just full of sort of . . . *sensible rantings*. When we actually did an interview with him he wrote the fact that he was coming down to London to talk to us and it was the first time I'd ever been in a gossip column. So obviously I'll wave a flag for him.

TONY LIVESEY: I've had feedback from friends who say they love Shaun's column, but what matters more to me is professional feedback. I also work for the *News Of The World*, and their senior journalists talk about how they always read Ryder's column and they love it. To me, that means even more than the average punter saying it.

However, despite his thriving journalistic career, Shaun Ryder's personal life was once again getting badly fucked up.

After leaving Too-Nice Tom's place, Shaun had moved into a rented gaff around the corner in Burnley in Carlton Road. The place was a pit. The house was a badly decayed three-storey, four-bedroom Victorian terrace without heating. Or, come to that, furniture. Naked bulbs hung from wire flexes over bare floorboards.

Shaun was living in one bare room on the second floor. It contained no bed but a mattress in one corner, a three-bar electric fire and a TV with a reception worse than Prince Philip would expect on a Chinese state visit.

The walls were woodchip, the ceiling cracked, the filthy grey carpet a mess of cigarette burns and ancient stains.

If the room looked bad before Shaun moved in, his efforts hardly improved it. Pot Noodle cartons and old chip wrappers soon became permanent features in his personal slum. Only the clobber hanging on the back wall sent by Admiral, Shaun's long-term sponsors, gave any impression of anything but abject misery and poverty.

Shaun spent his days – and nights – in this grotty gaff, huddled under the duvet with his new girlfriend, a Burnley lass of Swedish descent named Heidi. Her full name translated as Princess Happy Apple, but 'happy' wasn't a word which seemed very appropriate round at Carlton Road.

Heidi wasn't the only visitor to Carlton Road, though. It's hard for Shaun Ryder to be anonymous anywhere. People like Shaun are magnets who attract certain other sorts of people. Like honey pots attract bees, like dead flesh attracts flies, it was only a matter of time before the Burnley smack brigade got a sniff of where their prophet was staying and, like wise men, came bearing gifts.

So, inevitably, as local druggies and dealers heard of his presence in their town, they beat a path to his door. And away from Tom Bruggen, and despite his expensive stomach implants, Shaun fell back into drugs.

Different locals came and went, each addicted to their own particular poison. There was a weed man, a speed fiend, a crackhead, a smackhead, a Tamazi man, all bringing their own special offerings to share and to sell. On my weekly *Sport* visits I took my own gifts of wine, triple-strength lager and Chinese food, but every trip was finding Shaun worse than the week before.

And, inevitably, some of the more hardcore locals would come around to smoke smack or crack and Shaun would join in. Why not? He had nothing else to do. The music scene was behind him. There was nowt else to do now apart from get wasted and watch crap telly. Bereft of any routine other than waking and sleeping, he sank further into the abyss. The drugs came and went, as did the days.

The weeks ticked by. Too-Nice Tom was busy with his new baby and Shaun was sinking into his own little world. Anyone who knew him could see he was frustrated. He was tired of doing nothing, back in the bedsit-land twilight zone he'd inhabited fifteen years earlier in Little Hulton, Salford. He was bored, and when Shaun Ryder is bored, that means drugs. And lots of them.

Somehow we continued to knock up decent weekly columns together for the *Sport*, but Shaun was deteriorating rapidly. Other people also noticed him getting worse. It was kind of hard to miss.

TONY LIVESEY: When I first met Shaun, when he was staying at Too-Nice Tom's, he wasn't too bad. He was semi-alright. I mean, I'd heard all these stories about him being on drugs, right, but then I'd also heard these stories about him being one of the greatest musicians of the nineties and how he was going to do this and do that. So I took my wife round to Tom's and we had a big get-together and Shaun was telling all his showbiz stories. He was telling us how he knew Bono, and how Chris Evans used to send gifts over to his mansion in Ireland, and how he got £150,000 just for doing one gig. And so on. I was quite in awe, just a punter having dinner with Shaun Ryder.

Shaun was still in touch with reality then, because he could only drink four small cans of warm lager a day because he had these implants to get off the drugs. And I thought, he's fine. But then two or three months later when he'd moved out from Tom's, Shaun was a gibbering wreck. He was nearly dead.

He used to come into the *Sport* a lot, almost a fixture, and it was nice having him around. But then he started nicking things. He'd come in and, if you didn't know he was Shaun Ryder here on business, you'd think he was some lunatic who'd come to mug you and trash the place. I used to have to leave him in the foyer quite a lot.

One day I was in my office with him and I nipped out to make a brew. Shaun had come in trying to ponce some money, and there was a topless picture of Posh Spice in a frame on my wall. I came back in the office and Shaun said, 'Tony, I've got to go now,' and he had stuffed Posh Spice up his jumper. He was nicking it to try to sell it, and he really thought I wouldn't notice that my picture had gone and that the front of his jumper was all square.

I just felt really sorry for him. I couldn't say, 'For shame, Shaun, take Posh Spice from up your jumper.' Then he left, and went over to the brothel across the road. Whether he went for a wank, or whatever, I don't know, because I think he knew the woman who ran it. And I sent someone to the pub later to get the picture back off him.

I had one meeting with Shaun where he was practically a tramp. He had nothing, no cash. At the time I thought that as well as getting a decent columnist we were also doing a social service, and that if it wasn't for our money that he was getting he really would be dead. I'd never seen a man look so rough and still be alive.

Apart from maybe Shane McGowan.

As if Shaun wasn't suffering enough hardship already, Livesey then had to halve his weekly pay for the column. Lawyers representing Shaun's estranged partner Oriole contacted the *Sport* claiming that she was entitled to any money Shaun was being paid. His weekly pay for the *Daily Sport* column had to be halved after lawyers for Oriole filed a suit claiming she was entitled to the money. Livesey struck a deal.

TONY LIVESEY: Then we got sued by his wife for half the money. Her solicitors said, 'We believe you're paying Shaun Ryder, he owes us X amounts of pounds, stop employing him.' So I wrote a letter saying, 'What's the point in that? At least if Shaun agrees to pay you half then everyone gets something. Otherwise it's just stopping it for the sake of it.' So every week now his ex-wife gets half of his column.

On one occasion, Shaun wanted to visit the *Sport* and couldn't afford the cab fare from Burnley. He booked a cab anyway, and on arrival in Manchester, sent the cabbie into his friend's brothel over the road from the newspaper's office for payment. There was a happy ending as the cabbie emerged 45 minutes later with a big fat grin on his face and ready to take him back again.

However, one trip down to London, which Tony Livesey endured with Shaun, was a near-disaster – which somehow became a bizarre triumph:

TONY LIVESEY: We were publishing the *Sport*'s book, *Babes, Booze, Orgies and Aliens*. Shaun was tied in to help launch it and *Esquire* magazine had agreed to come along and do a feature on the launch, and Shaun was fucking wrecked. I knew it was going to be a nightmare from the minute I got on the train with him in Manchester. He was so drugged-up he was just asleep for thirty-minute bursts, then he'd wake up for two minutes, say something I couldn't understand and then go back to sleep again.

Shaun did a drug deal on the train when we got into Euston. I was just sat there, and this is the honest-to-God's truth and a sign of my naivety. Shaun got on the phone to his mate and he was talking about how he was going to get this gear. I didn't know they were talking about drugs. Shaun said down the phone, 'Who's the Queen's eldest son?' and I didn't think he knew, and I was trying to tell him it was Charles.

Of course he was talking about cocaine, but I didn't have a clue and I was so embarrassed about that. See, Shaun came from a world I didn't know. I knew he'd be good for the paper and wanted that raw edge, but I don't know that sort of world. Anyway, then we arrived with a view to going out on the piss and launching the book. We went to this bar in Soho and Shaun had had loads of free clothes delivered because he seems to do that wherever he goes. He gives his old stuff away and gets re-dressed again which he did in this pub. Then he just ran off. He just disappeared.

So I was sat there for hours with these people from *Esquire*, who were all twiddling their thumbs. We all got well drunk. Then Shaun turned back up with Chris Evans. That's the kind of pulling power Shaun's got. I'd always wanted to meet Chris Evans and Shaun just walked in with him because he'd met him in the street near Evans' offices. So he brought Evans out on the piss and we just went on the beer all day. Chris was buying all the beers and Shaun was on treble vodkas.

That seemed to be how Shaun was living his life at that time. He was mixing with celebrities one minute, and then back home in Burnley, at Carlton Road, he was just a wreck. I went round his flat one night for something and he was fucking *gone*. It wouldn't have surprised me at the time if someone had called me and said, 'Shaun's dead'.

Shaun was living this bizarre lifestyle in this weird Burnley terraced house which was completely empty. He was losing it badly. At one point he wanted me to sue his local newsagent over his paper bill! They tried to charge him for his newspapers and he said the *Sport* was paying on account. There was this huge scene in the newsagent's with Shaun threatening to sue this poor bloke. The other funny thing from those days is that Shaun Ryder, the wild man of rock who was the spokesman for a generation and set all the trends for drugs, used to do his drinking in a Wacky Warehouse in Burnley. It was his nearest pub, but it was also a wacky warehouse for kids with climbing frames and swings. That's where he used to go to do his drinking.

There was this surreal scene of kids in party hats singing, 'Happy Birthday', and Shaun Ryder sitting there having a drink.

Shaun continued to alternate his day-to-day life of squalor in Burnley with high-profile celebrity events. His next reappearance on the public stage came in November 1998 when Radio One's Jo Whiley invited him on to her TV show where various celebs gathered on sofas each week to analyse the latest single releases. Shaun's appearance didn't run smoothly, and he nearly didn't make it on to the air at all at one point because of his refusal to hide the brand name on his baseball cap.

He proved he still had his sense of humour, but Whiley, a die-hard Mondays fan who had known Shaun for years, could tell things were not all well on the Ryder front.

JO WHILEY: I've known Shaun for ages, and met him once during his Radio One Roadshow Ibiza jaunt. It was on the beach. I think it was Cafe Del Mar and it was one of those terrific Ibiza sunsets and everyone was hanging out chilling. I walked along and Shaun was there surrounded by a group of girls, literally holding court and entertaining everybody.

He turned round and he was like, 'Oh, Jo,' and we had a chat there and he was telling me all about the film he was making. He asked me to play a part in it, which was to be the mother of a group of teenage girls or something, and I said, 'Thanks, Shaun, what a compliment.'

Shaun is a major character, who obviously goes through different cycles in his life. There are some times when he's really on it, and others when he's kind of struggling. But every time I've met him, whenever, he's always been completely engaging and very funny and very witty, even if he's in a bit of a fog and he's having a tough time. The wit is still there and that's what happened when he came on the TV show.

The show was funny but it was also very hard work. He was on with Huey from Fun Loving

Criminals and they'd been socialising quite a bit before the show and came on a bit worse for wear. Shaun was so unpredictable I didn't know how he was going to react to anything that was going on. There was a bit of a battle with the producer, who kept saying into my earpiece, 'Can you get Shaun to turn his hat round because it's got a brand name on it.'

So I said, 'Shaun, do you mind just turning your hat round, so we can't see the brand name.'

He just went, 'I ain't turning me hat round.' So I spoke to the producer and said Shaun wants his hat round this way, but they were saying, 'No! He has to turn his hat round the other way.'

So again I had to ask, 'Shaun, would you really mind turning your hat round?'

'I ain't turning me hat round.' We had this feud for about five or ten minutes, and the producer was going 'Well, we can't do the show if he doesn't turn his hat round.' And in the end Shaun just cracked a smile and turned his hat round. It was like we reached a compromise somewhere along the line, but he knew exactly what was going on. It was very funny, but I was in a very difficult position.

Also he came up with this classic line. He was talking about Kate Bush and saying how he was absolutely in love with her and thought she was the best thing ever. He said he went to her gig and went out the back for a cig and there was Kate Bush having a cig as well. He couldn't believe there was Kate Bush having a cig, and he said this classic line about seeing Kate having a 'bifta'.

And at the time I was seven months pregnant and he was trying to convince me that it was good to smoke dope for babies. He was fairly evangelical about it. He told me cigarettes were a no-no but smoking dope was good.

I think he was going through a bit of a tough time. But I just really, really wanted him on the show because I knew that he'd be smart.

After Jo's show Shaun went back to Burnley, back to the people he didn't really know and back to his grotesque rented accommodation. The local druggies continued to turn up and he continued sampling their wares. It was ironic that he'd originally gone to Burnley to rewrite his life because this was now the same tired, repetitive old script.

It was boredom that had first created Happy Mondays. They were five lads stuck in a rut, bored to their back teeth and with the prospect of spending the rest of their lives earning a low wage in a crap job or turning to crime to make ends meet. Now Shaun was back in a rut and bored shitless. The more bored he got, the more off his head he got. The more off his head he got, the more unpredictable he became.

One night after things got a bit on top of him in Burnley, he had stayed at his parents' home in Worsley, just a few yards from where Manchester United players David Beckham and Ryan Giggs were living at the time. As Shaun stared at his parents' telly, a state-of-the-art 40″ Ni-Cam job, he decided he wanted to take it back to Burnley with him.

In his confused and addled head, this made sense. He'd bought the TV for his folks back when things were going well, and now he was deep in the shit he wanted some payback. Needless to say, this led to a big row. A massive fucking row, in fact, which spilled into the street until Shaun's dad, Horseman, finally disappeared back inside the house and came out carrying the telly.

Shaun's dad is only a little bloke, although he's pretty stocky, and the telly was almost bigger than him. Shaun was trying to stuff it into the boot of a car when a punch-up broke out between him, his brother Paul and his dad. The telly, which was teetering on the edge of the boot, fell to the ground and smashed on the pavement. The fight was broken up by Linda, Shaun's mum. It's sad to report that Shaun hasn't spoken to his dad since.

So Shaun retreated to Burnley, where things were turning sourer by the minute. Rumours were flying around town about what he was up to. Some may have been started by accident, but it seemed at the time that someone with a bitter tongue and a twisted mind was stirring up some serious shit for him. Depending on who you talked to at that time, he was either hanging out with the wrong crowd, being watched by the police, or handing out sweets to kids outside the gates of the local primary school.

The last one is complete and utter bollocks, of course, but it was actually said by somebody or other. It may have been someone who had an axe to grind, or even someone attempting to make a joke. However it helped turn Shaun's name in Burnley to shit.

There's no denying he was down at this point. He was skint, because all his money was tied up in Oriole's name. And now some arsewipes were taking

Shaun for a whipping boy and spreading these lies about him.

Shaun Ryder was a fallen idol. A pop star on skid row – and one within hitting distance. There's always someone ready to take a pop at you for what you were. One night Ryder was out at a local club just for something to do when a yob surrounded by half-a-dozen mates waltzed up and punched him in the eye. Shaun staggered and the bloke melted away into the crowd.

Normally, this would have led to a full-on battle, with chairs, bottles and tables flying in every direction as Ryder went after the geezer with fists flailing, regardless of whether he had a chance or not. That Shaun let this wanker get away with his nasty assault was indicative of his current depression.

In fact, Shaun's masterly response to the attack was a classic example of the pen being mightier than the sword. The next week, in his *Daily Sport* column, Shaun referred to the club. He said he'd had such a good time there that he'd invited all his mates from Salford along that week, and could guarantee they'd have a 'smashing' time.

Shaun was laughing when he said this to me, but it was clear what he was implying; Salford were coming down for revenge, and there was going to be big trouble. Of course Salford weren't *really* coming down. But that didn't matter. Word soon arrived at Carlton Road that the terrified thug had left Burnley in a big hurry. He wouldn't be seen again for months.

It was around this time, October 1998, that the ridiculous and far-fetched idea of a Happy Mondays reunion was first floated. Unknown to me, there had been discussions ongoing between Shaun, Paul and promoter Simon Moran about the possibility of the band reuniting. Shaun had categorically knocked the idea back, saying he'd had enough of that scene to last him ten lifetimes.

On October 16, Shaun announced in his weekly *Sport* column:

IT'S GREAT TALKING STRAIGHT

I've been offered megabucks to put the Mondays back together and do a few gigs in England and a few festivals. But unfortunately it's not going to happen. I want out of that game for a while. That's why I packed Black Grape in. I want to concentrate on writing, doing movies, and being a journalist.

Well, as for writing and movies went he still had *Molly's Idle Ways* in the pipeline. He had also made an hilarious appearance in the ill-fated bastardised Hollywood version of *The Avengers* with Uma Thurman and Ralph Fiennes. Shaun had played a mop-top evil henchman alongside Eddie Izzard, who shot at Fiennes with an Uzi and piloted radio-controlled killer bees towards their bowler-hatted quarry. He also took a bashing from Steed's umbrella after trying to stick him with a bowie knife.

So on October 16, Shaun had announced that he wouldn't re-form the Mondays, no matter how big the incentive. However, six weeks down the line, he'd had the chance to do a lot of thinking. The club attack had made Shaun realise how much he needed to get of Burnley. He was 37 years old, going nowhere, still taking shitloads of class A drugs and still poverty-stricken, with all his money from the *Sport* and all other sources being tied up in the legal wrangling with his ex-partner Oriole. Nicholl and Dime were also still hovering and threatening legal action.

And, most pressingly, there was the business of the taxman. The Inland Revenue had just hit Shaun Ryder with a bill for more than £200,000 of unpaid income tax on his Black Grape earnings. Shaun was truly and regally fucked. He had to do something.

There was only one thing he *could* do.

The final change of heart came completely out of the blue, on a cold November Tuesday night. It had been a crazy night like many others at Carlton Road.

The announcement was made to a bleary-eyed hack. Me. I'd spent the last five hours sat in a room full of strangers, watching a TV set with more snow on it than Al Pacino's mirror in *Scarface*. I'd been waiting for Shaun, who was on a bit of a mad one, to come out of a back room and do his column.

We finally got around to it, and I'd got plenty of the usual stuff to fill it with. He'd given me his take on current affairs, the regular 'Single Of The Week' and of course the famous 'Celebrity Tits Out' slot where Shaun invites various famous women to take a picture of their own breasts and send it in to him. We'd had a smoke and a joke, a couple of drinks, and I was on my way down the uncarpeted staircase to the hall where a freezing wind was whistling through the letterbox.

Shaun came to the top of the staircase to see me out, and as I hit the bottom stair he shouted down to me, almost as an afterthought: '*Oh, and by the way . . . I'm going to get the band back together.*'

3. TAX BLOW SPARKS BAD BOYS' RETURN

Bez moves to Royston Vasey, stoned man sets self on fire, Paul Ryder 'forgets' solo album, Bez confounded by doorhandles, Paul eats dog bone, Shaun decides to re-form Mondays, tells Sport before telling band members.

The idea of re-forming Happy Mondays arrived in Shaun's mind during those low months at the end of '98 by a somewhat circuitous route. The seed had originally been planted by concert promoter Simon Moran of SJM Promotions. He had suggested re-forming the band to Paul, when he bumped into him outside a gig in Warrington in August of that year.

> **PAUL RYDER:** I'd gone to see Fun Loving Criminals in Warrington. It was a mega gig. After the gig I came out and there was a little burger joint across the street. So I was in there getting something to eat when Simon Moran pulled up and jumped out of his car. I hadn't seen him for years.
>
> I said, 'Alright, Simon?' And Simon said, 'Fucking hell, I was just thinking about you! Do you fancy going on tour for the Mondays?' I didn't know what to say, so I said, 'I don't really fancy playing fucking gigs at the Boardwalk any more. Where were you thinking of putting the gigs on?' And he said, 'Manchester Evening News Arena.' I said, 'You're off your fucking head.'

Then he said, 'And the SECC in Glasgow and a couple of nights at Brixton Academy.' I said, 'You really are off your fucking head, Simon!'

I told him I'd talk to Shaun. But I didn't like the idea.

Paul spoke to Shaun and Shaun emphatically knocked the idea back, leading to the column in the *Sport* mentioned previously. However, Moran was persistent. His relationship with the band had been a long-standing one – and he wanted to re-ignite it.

Moran had first seen Happy Mondays play fourteen years earlier at Manchester's Boardwalk club, where they hired rehearsal rooms. One year later he was putting on their gigs alongside baggy Scouse band The Farm. Moran had continued to promote the Mondays until he was unceremoniously dumped in 1988 by the then manager Nathan McGough.

A slight, bespectacled, tanned man with pinched features, a fetish for jogging and a face like a loveable hamster, Moran had also been the sole promoter behind Black Grape before their untimely demise. Now, in late 1998, the Mondays had been on his thoughts for a while.

SIMON MORAN: I thought a Mondays reunion would work. As a promoter, I knew there'd be a demand in the market for people to see them. Shaun had kept in the public spotlight, so I just thought, why not do it? I'd always found them OK to deal with. So when I bumped into Paul outside a gig in Warrington, I asked him. He seemed surprised, but he said he'd speak to his brother.

Despite the initial knock-back, Moran persisted. He contacted Paul Ryder again a couple of weeks later and outlined exactly what the tour would entail – a short series of big dates in arenas around the UK. The money side was tempting. Paul spoke to Shaun again.

PAUL RYDER: I phoned our kid again and told him what Simon had said this time around. Shaun said, 'What, get the old firm together again?' And I said, 'Yeah.' And Shaun paused, then said, 'Well, never say never.'

Shaun found himself pondering the idea. Deciding he quite fancied it, he dropped his casual bombshell on me in Burnley. Then – and this is archetypally Ryder – he announced the big news in the *Daily Sport* without bothering to tell his brother, Gaz Whelan, or indeed anybody.

IT'S GREAT TALKING STRAIGHT

The big news this week, dudes, is I'm re-forming the Mondays for a few one-off gigs.

I'm starting to miss a bit of the buzz of doing the music. We've been offered three gigs – Manchester, Amsterdam and London. And I'm going to get the band back together for them.

Now I don't have to have the full line-up. For a start the keyboard player's out and the guitarist's out. It'll be Gaz the original drummer, original me, original bass player Paul Ryder, and I don't know where Bez stands, he'll probably want about £27 million for the three gigs.

My PR person Anton Brooks wants it to work too, and with some cool DJs it would be really f***ing sorted.

I can't do touring any more. It really pisses me off and you get bled dry. How do they expect you to get on a plane, six o'clock in the morning, do a twelve-hour flight to LA, get off, go and do interviews, then take a six-hour flight to your gig in New York? I'm fed up of it.

But I could really go for one of those one-off, greatest hits sort of gigs, plus a few tracks from the up-and-coming movie *Molly's Idle Ways*.

The Mondays' music has a whole new audience now, kids who are twenty were just ten when it was all going on.

And if it all goes to plan we should have dates sorted for around Christmas time, or early New Year.

It might have made more sense for Shaun to consult his brother and Gaz Whelan before using the pages of the national press to announce the reunion – because both had very good reasons for not wanting to do it.

Paul had had a very bad time since the band ended. For one thing, the Mondays had left him a physical and mental wreck. There had been times over the last six years when he was arguably in an even worse state than his brother had found himself in in Burnley.

Paul Ryder had developed a taste for crack after the original Mondays trip to America in the late eighties. After the Caribbean, though, he'd developed a full-scale heroin addiction. He'd also hooked up with Astrella, another daughter of Donovan and the sister of

Shaun's estranged partner Oriole. He even made an album with Astrella, although he was so smacked out at the time that he has no memory of it.

PAUL RYDER: Yeah, we made an album which I've totally forgotten about. I was so heavily into my drug usage at the time. Apparently it's alright, but I haven't heard it since the day I split up with Astrella, which was five years ago. It was just me and Astrella and a couple of engineers. I've heard it's, er, quite good, but I really couldn't tell you.

After splitting from Astrella in the mid-nineties Paul had got even more dependent on smack to help ease the pain of their separation. His use had become prodigious, until he'd spiralled into depression and finally suffered a full nervous breakdown.

Paul spent time at Meadowbrook, a hospital for mental illnesses, before he'd been moved to Trafford General Hospital, where he sat in the casualty department with a dog bone between his teeth, growling at members of staff. He'd been quickly admitted for treatment, and underwent a series of brain scans. He was completely adrift – yet still had the presence of mind to arrange for regular deliveries of skag to be brought to the hospital for him.

PAUL RYDER: I was fucked in my head, but I had enough brain cells left to get the gear delivered to me while I was in hospital.

Paul was discharged from Trafford after a routine hospital test had revealed he was still taking the drug.

Sergio Bondioni

'There isn't a comparison for them in rock'n'roll. It's not Jagger and Richards, because Jagger sings and Richards plays guitar... For most people their biggest value is not the value of the songwriting or the value of the performer, their biggest value is as cultural icons' – Tony Wilson

WANTED

MISSING ON IBIZA

The Mondays get stoned in Greenhouse

HORSE

ROW

WAGS

BEN

GAZ

Left: The *Sport* resorts to desperate measures to locate their missing columnist. 'Shaun was going face-first in his soup every dinnertime' said Livesey.

X + ROW

Shaun gets Nuts trapped in vice, twists melons, as lesbo sex orgy erupts in top London hotel. The world yawns.

Paul Stanley

Carl Royle

Top left: Bez, Bobby Gillespie and Wags
Top right: Bez
Middle left: Wags
Middle right: Nuts with Shed 7
Bottom: Happy Mondays 2000

Despite feuding brothers, lurking bailiffs, charred feet, Shaun's nerves, Bez's puke, autocued lyrics and unprecedented guest-list abuse, the Mondays' reunion tour was a resounding triumph.

Paul Stanley

Paul Stanley (and over)

'The gig was fantastic. The Mondays could actually play! They had become a better band and it was a bit of a shock really. I remember being on the phone to my mate and saying "Listen to this!" and holding my phone up so he could hear'
– Keith Allen

Colour shots: Brian Sweeney

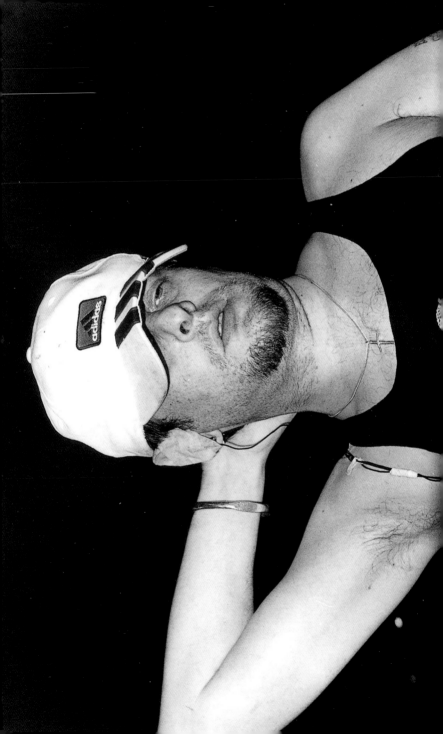

He'd returned to his parents' house in Worsley, where he finally made the decision to go cold turkey and get clean.

> **PAUL RYDER:** I decided I didn't want to go back to the nuthouse and I didn't want a heroin habit, so there was only one thing for it.

So Paul had spent 1998 with his parents, grown a beard, watched TV – until Shaun turned up from Burnley to reclaim it – and slowly weaned himself off heroin. He'd also stayed best pals with Gaz Whelan, who came to visit him every day while he was recovering.

This was the state that Paul had arguably gotten into through being in Happy Mondays. He wasn't sure he wanted the chance to do it all again.

> **PAUL RYDER:** I was actually in a really bad way when I met Simon Moran. I'd just come out of another fucking mental institute and was slowly getting better when this offer came along. I'd been six years out of the business, and this came along and knocked me sideways.

Initially, like Shaun, Paul had dismissed the reunion idea out of hand. Then he decided to tell Gaz Whelan about it. Paul and Gaz had stayed tight since the Mondays' split. As well as visiting the recuperating Paul on a daily basis, Gaz had also recently talked Paul into taking a sound engineers' course at a local college to help him get back into the swing of things.

Gaz, if anything, was even less pleased to hear the news than Paul. After the Mondays split, he'd found himself adrift. He'd struggled from musical project to project and felt his life had lost its focus, which in a way it had. It was only through his will-power that he'd survived the ordeal without collecting a serious addiction. This was no small feat, given he'd joined the band at fifteen and had Paul and Shaun as role models for his formative years.

Just recently, though, Whelan had made some life decisions. He didn't know what he wanted to do, but he *did* know he didn't want anything at all to do with the music industry. He was as horrified as Paul at Moran's idea. Of course, there was the chance to make some money again. But he thought the Mondays had done a lot of damage to his life. Once bitten, twice shy.

GAZ WHELAN: After the Mondays split, I didn't do anything for about six months. Then PD and Mark Day got a band together and asked if I wanted to do stuff with them. It was called Delicious. Andy Rourke from The Smiths was in it. Then Mark Day left, then PD left, so me and Andy decided to get a band together, which we did. But I never enjoyed it. I'd been in the Mondays since I was fifteen, and playing with a different singer and bass player was really weird and I never got into it. It was wrong from day one. But it went on for about three years or something, then I packed it in and didn't do anything.

I didn't see any of the Mondays for ages. I didn't see Shaun for years. I've only seen Mark Day once ever since – in Swinton, when Black

Grape had just got to Number One with the album and I'd seen them at the Apollo. I told him they were really good. He said he hadn't even heard of them.

After Delicious, I fucked off to America for six months. I travelled across the country, and while I was there I decided what it was I wanted to do – and what I wanted to do was to have nothing to do with music. Then I got back, saw Horse [Paul Ryder] and he said Simon Moran had been phoning him asking about doing tours, and I was like, 'Aw, Horse, I've just decided I'm not going to do anything.' He was like, 'Well, we'll see what he's got to say.'

Gaz and Paul, like Shaun, had initially been convinced it was a ridiculous idea to reunite the Mondays. They knew loads of reasons why they shouldn't do it. They remembered how messy it had got the last time and had vowed not to make the same mistakes again. They'd made their decision. It was final.

But then slowly, fatally, they began to change their minds. Paul and Gaz started chipping away at the other's inhibitions and doubts. Despite themselves – and both had serious misgivings – they started to warm to the idea.

Out came the old photos and the old tapes. The pair cracked a couple of beers and began to reminisce about old times. The memories came flooding back: Barcelona, Paris, the Manchester G-MEX shows, baggy trousers and free beer.

GAZ WHELAN: Paul felt the same as me. He wasn't giving much away but I think he was excited underneath it all. He kept digging up tapes we'd done when I was fifteen, Paul was seventeen, and Shaun was nineteen. Then he was talking about how good we were and how we used to have a laugh although we were skint.

I think he was convincing himself.

PAUL RYDER: Me and Gaz sat in my mum and dad's house and put some tunes on. We played a couple off *Yes Please*, a couple off *Pills 'N' Thrills* . . . and a couple of the re-mixes. I'd never actually done it before, believe it or not. Never actually sat down and listened to our own tunes, my own records. And suddenly we were saying, 'Fucking hell, we were a good band!' We realised there were people out there who hadn't seen us. And I always thought we'd split up too soon anyway. So yeah, that was the moment that made up my mind.

Once he'd made his fateful decision, Shaun Ryder told everybody who asked him why he was re-forming the band the same reason. It was because he'd been hit with this stinker of a bill from the taxman. He had to find £200,000 and there was nowhere else it was going to come from. But was this the full reason? Why the fuck *was* Shaun Ryder re-forming Happy Mondays?

SHAUN: When people ask me why I did it, I always say, 'Tax bill.' It's dead easy. But it wasn't really just because of the tax bill. It just seemed right to do it.

I got hit for a load of things all at once, right. I was coming out of a seven-year relationship, which cost me. Things in Burnley had turned to shit. Plus I had a rest from music after Black Grape, and I was doing other things like putting films together and stuff like that. It just seemed the time was right.

This wasn't the whole story, though. Pardon the cliché but Shaun Ryder is an artist. OK, he's a blag artist and a piss artist, but he's still an artist. And if artists aren't creating they're dying. Right now, fucked in Burnley, Shaun was engaged on a mission to self-destruct.

And the taxman gave him the perfect reason to be a glorious hypocrite. Now he could get the band back together for exactly the same reason he'd broken it up six years earlier – the money. But behind this simple reason was one far more complex. He needed to do it to save himself.

He'd had enough. Shaun could have lived a life as a normal person if the band hadn't taken off. Maybe he'd have been a crook, a cook or a street cleaner. However, the chance to do anything normal had gone out of the window the first time he was recognised in the street. He'd discovered – and maybe the punch on the jaw in the club had been the final evidence – that he simply couldn't go back to living anonymously.

For better or worse, he was Shaun Ryder, pop star. And if that was the case, well, he might as well make some money out of it.

Arrangements were made for Shaun to finally quit Burnley and move back to Manchester. His hellish time in east Lancashire was, thankfully, over. Shaun moved in with his long-time pal Gary (G-man) Marsden, in Chorlton.

Shaun had made it absolutely clear to Moran from the start that there was no way he would allow his sworn enemies, Mark 'Moose/Cowhead' Day and Paul 'PD' Davis, back into the fold. They'd said they'd never work with him again – and he intended to hold them to it.

Unfortunately, in the time lapse between Shaun writing in the *Daily Sport* that he'd decided to re-form the band and actually telling the other band members, Gaz had a chance meeting with PD.

GAZ WHELAN: I bumped into PD just before everything happened. He was in town and we said hello and had a chat. He seemed OK. He was at college doing a computer course. Then he called me close to Christmas and said, 'I've heard this rumour that Simon Moran's talking about getting the band together and touring and all that.'

I said – and at the time it was a totally honest answer – 'Well, yeah, I've heard the rumour, but I don't think anything is going to come of it.' And then the very next day Simon set up the meeting for me, Paul and Shaun, because Shaun had said 'Yes' to Simon and written it in the *Sport* without telling me and Paul.

Afterwards, I thought, I bet PD thinks I was lying, but Simon genuinely called me the day after I'd spoken to PD. It was just one of those weird things.

One minor problem remained – Horseman's attitude towards the reunion. Derek Ryder, Shaun and Paul's dad, was a former stand-up comedian who was once beaten in a talent competition by a pre-pubescent Lisa Stansfield, and who'd gone everywhere with Mondays the first time around. Derek had made sure the original Mondays had food and drink and arrived at gigs on time, and generally looked after them.

Horseman was totally opposed to the Mondays re-forming without Mark Day and Paul Davis, and let everyone know it. 'I don't want anything to do with it,' he said. 'I think getting the Mondays back together is a terrible idea. People say, "It'll be great, I never saw the Mondays first time round." But I tell them they're not going to see the Mondays. It's not the Mondays without Moose on guitar and PD on keyboards.'

PAUL DAVIS: I think I read about it in the paper. I walked into a newsagent's and someone said, 'Oh, you're getting back together are you?' I said 'Not at all,' you know what I mean? I'm the one who left originally, I mean I'm the one who split the rotten apple. That was it, I just walked into a newsagent's and found out for myself, I was just like, 'Oh God, there's nothing better than a good old bloated fucking pop star is there?' Get the last tour out of them that you can, squeeze every last fucking lyric out of him. And every bit of music out of the musicians. Sad, very sad.

I wasn't expecting to be asked back. Fucking hell, I was the one who'd fucking fucked them off. Shaun's too proud, I'm too proud. I never want to see or speak to him again.

Shaun still wasn't talking to his dad after the broken TV incident and didn't give a fuck what he thought.

Paul, though, was staying with his parents after his drug-related illness, and would have loved his old man's thumbs-up for the re-union. Eventually he had to accept that he wasn't going to get it.

GAZ WHELAN: For a while Paul was saying he didn't know if he should do it, because his dad was against it, and Paul really wanted the blessing of his dad. So I thought that was it, he wouldn't do it. Then one day Paul called me up and said, 'Oh, I want to do it, whatever my dad says. I wish I could've had me dad's blessing but I still want to do it.'

So Simon Moran arranged a meeting with the two Ryder brothers and Gaz Whelan in a Manchester bar. This proved fairly straightforward. All parties were up for the reunion, and everyone agreed for one reason or another that Mark and PD would not be invited to rejoin the line-up. They discussed potential replacements. Shaun decided that his former Black Grape mate Paul (Wags) Wagstaff would be an ideal substitute for Cowhead on guitar. Simon suggested that Ben Leach, former keyboard player with The Farm, could take over from PD on keyboards and also play the role of musical director. Both ideas were carried unanimously.

SHAUN: I was asked by Simon Moran who I thought would be a good guitarist after Mark Day. They said, 'Have you got any objections to Wags?' I said, 'No, he'll fit in perfectly.' If there's anybody that would fit in with us naturally, working in our uniquely lazy style, it was Wags. He'd been in Black Grape. He was right.

PAUL RYDER: Mark Day was never in the equation. PD was a funny guy and I knew I'd miss his sense of humour but we had to get it right. It had to be the right line-up with no mistakes, and Cowhead and PD had gone on record in the papers years ago saying they'd never work with the Ryder brothers again. So it was his choice. I missed PD's sense of humour – but that's all I missed.

The reunion line-up was now in place, with one major and glaring omission. Nobody knew what Bez's views on the subject were and how keen he would be on being involved. He hadn't left the Mondays on the best of terms and, although there had been a minor *rapprochement* since, he and Shaun had fallen out big time at the end of Black Grape.

In fact, a lot had happened to Bez since the end of Black Grape. His relationship with his long-time girlfriend and mother of his two sons Deborah Faulkner went through a rocky patch when he was severely caning the hard drugs. However, the couple finally managed to resolve their differences, and Bez began playing at happy families rather than Happy Mondays.

Deborah had helped Bez to write his autobiography, *Freaky Dancing*, which had been published to mixed but generally affectionate reviews. The book had appeared in the summer of 1998, around the same time that Shaun started writing for the *Daily Sport,* and Shaun had used his column to express his doubts about the veracity of its contents. In fact, he accused Bez of talking a load of bollocks.

SHAUN: Let's just say I was amazed to find out it was me that did all those things, and never Bez.

However, the book's launch was a major media event, attended by luminaries like former Clash singer Joe Strummer.

JOE STRUMMER: There was a huge piss-up at the launch party, and afterwards there was a bit of acid going around. Bez told me later that when he and his mates got back to their hotel, which was a shrine to modernity and minimalism, they had to spend the night in the corridor because they couldn't find the minimalist door handles to their rooms.

Bez had also followed Shaun into the journalistic world. He'd been commissioned by laddish monthly men's magazine *Front* to write a monthly column called 'Bez Sez'.

BEZ: The magazine phoned me up one day and asked if I wanted to go for a night out in Leeds with them. They have this medal they give to *Front* heroes, and that night they asked me if I wanted to write a monthly column. I said I didn't think I could write something every month. I still fucking don't know if I can or not, but it's better than selling drugs, or shoplifting, or signing on the dole or owt. And it only takes ten minutes.

I often find myself doing mad bits of work. People phone me up asking me if I want to do things, and more often than not I say yeah.

Front promised Bez £1 per word for his monthly article:

BEZ: The first month I wrote them about five thousand words, hoping they'd pay me £5,000, but they were having none of it.

When it came down to it, there were many reasons why Bez might not want to reunite with a band which had split so acrimoniously. He was still living with Deborah in their cottage in the remote village near to Glossop, although at the time he and Debs weren't getting on and she had temporarily moved out. Simon Moran said that he would try to contact the bug-eyed dancer.

GAZ WHELAN: We had the meeting with Shaun, Paul and Simon but nobody knew what was happening with Bez. Simon said he'd get in touch with him and get it sorted. Then Simon called us all and said, 'Bez doesn't want to do it.' He called him a few times over three or four weeks. He just wasn't interested.

SHAUN: I could understand Bez not wanting to do it, because our kid, Mark Day, Paul Davis and Gaz treated him pretty disgustingly at the end of the Mondays. They treated Bez pretty crap. He might not have written songs or played an instrument, but he did his job, which was to get massive publicity, and he never got the respect he deserved for it. I could understand why he was fucked off and didn't want to come back.

Shaun, typically, had also gone public with his reservations about Bez. Shaun and Bez still hadn't properly buried that hatchet since the Black Grape split, and Shaun made a point of saying publicly that the reunion tour would go ahead whether or not their trademark freaky dancer was along for the ride.

The Mondays could have re-formed without Bez, obviously. They'd have sounded exactly the same. But they still knew they needed him. A plan was hatched.

GAZ WHELAN: Paul Ryder phoned me one day and said he had just spoken to Bez and it didn't look like he was having it. So Horse said, 'We're going to have to go to Glossop.' I said, 'When?' He said, 'Right now. Tonight.' It was fucking freezing.

Bez's Glossop cottage is the last place you'd expect to find the most famous wide-eyed manic face of the acid house era living. It's on a quiet street, on a quiet hillside, in a quiet town. The inside walls are pastel and the furniture Mexican pine. Bez has even converted the loft into a room for his two sons to play in, with glorious views across the Pennines. You can see sheep from his kitchen window and there are flowers in the fireplace.

It's about 30 miles from central Manchester to the tiny Derbyshire town which is now home to the

Ecstasy generation's gangly guru. Paul and Gaz set off there in an old Ford Fiesta with the sole intention of persuading their former buddy to come back into the band. It was just getting dark when the pair arrived to find Bez sat in the front room of his house with two pals having a smoke.

'I'm not fucking doing it,' Bez said immediately.

'Let's go to the pub and talk about it,' said Paul.

GAZ: So me and Paul drove up to Glossop to see Bez. We went to his house and he was in there. We hadn't seen him for years. I'd just seen him the once, a year earlier. I'd been crossing the road and he was driving a car. He'd told me he'd park and see me in the pub, but he never did. He just drove off.

We tried to talk to him, but he was adamant he wasn't doing it. So we went to the pub and me and Horse were talking to him for hours. We told him we weren't going to let it be like cabaret and that we thought we should go for it. After three hours he still wasn't sure. At the end of it he was still saying he wasn't having it but we had the feeling that he'd been swayed.

BEZ: To be truthful I can't remember how I first heard about the plans to get the Mondays back together. I'd heard rumours about it for months. People were saying to me, 'I hear Happy Mondays are re-forming'. And I'd just say, Well, if they are I don't know about it.' But I think the first I properly heard about it was that night when Horse and Gaz came up.

I was sat in my house with a few of my mates all getting stoned. I couldn't really be arsed with Horse and Gaz coming up, but they turned up and we ended up going to the boozer. We got fucking steaming, fucking flying drunk and argued the toss. I gave them a million fucking reasons why I didn't want to do it, and only one reason why I did – and that was money.

They had decided they really wanted to do it. Gaz's argument was, if we didn't do it now we couldn't do it in another ten years' time because we'd all be in wheelchairs. But I was adamant. One, I didn't want it to turn into cabaret, and two, I don't like working for smackheads. I didn't want to do it.

A smackhead's always a smackhead at the end of the day. He's clean as long as he's not taking smack but that temptation's there all the time. I wasn't convinced that there was no smack culture in the Mondays. Basically I couldn't be arsed knocking around with a load of junkies doing my fucking head in. That was my argument, basically.

The lot of us ended up getting blind drunk. It was getting really silly. And then the problem with the bog ceiling happened.

There is some dispute over exactly what caused the damage to the ceiling of the pub toilet in Bez's local, a few hundred yards from his Glossop cottage, on that emotional and eventful night. The pub landlord, who banned Bez from the establishment for a long while afterwards, claimed that Bez had punched holes in the ceiling. Bez, naturally, had another story.

BEZ: There was a few holes in the bog ceiling of our local, and we were getting blamed for it. We were saying, 'No fucking way, it wasn't us! It was some geezer who come through looking like he was on steroids!' But they didn't believe us.

PAUL RYDER: Me, Gaz and Bez got completely arseholed in Bez's local pub, yeah. We got completely bladdered in this little village. It was a really good night. And Bez got banned from his local pub as well. He was that excited that he went to the toilet in the pub and jumped up and down punching the ceiling in, and shouting, 'Yeah, we're all back together!' Although he says he didn't.

Bez's part in the pub ceiling disaster was somewhat suspicious, particularly as an hour earlier he'd been observed deliberately feeding three plastic logs on to the 'living flame' fire in the boozer.

GAZ: It was a really strange evening. After three hours in the pub we went out to the car and had a drive with him. Me, Horse and Bez just bonded again. It was like we were on tour again, and as though nothing had happened.

At the end of the evening Bez gave us both a hug and said he'd think about it but he still wasn't sure. He said, 'I want to do it for you,' but he was still worried it would turn out like some cabaret.

Paul and Gaz drove off into the night, but Bez's evening wasn't over yet. When he got home a riot ensued. His local Glossop mates had stayed in his cottage getting stoned, and Bez suddenly glimpsed through his alcohol and hash haze, in the charmingly subtle way in which, say, lightning communes with golfers, how to celebrate meeting the old gang again. He decided to ride his motorbike through the ground floor of his house.

Bez kick-started the machine in the dining room, and did several circuits of the dining table before heading out of the French windows into his garden to disturb the rhododendrons. His neighbours threatened to call the police. Bez suggested that they might possibly want to go fuck themselves.

> **BEZ:** Debs had left me for a while at the time because I was always being out of order. I was never coming home and staying out too many nights and getting off it. So I had the whole house to myself, and I kept my motorbike in the back room when she wasn't around. I think that's another of the reasons she left. It's in my mate's garage now.
>
> So me and my mates carried on getting pissed and I ended up riding my bike round the dining room. The neighbours were fucking coming in trying to tell us to shut it. We were just being totally fucking mad, come to think about it.

As the mayhem developed, one of Bez's extraordinarily stoned mates had an idea to develop the scene. This idea was slightly less sharp but even more dangerous than Bez's. It was an idea that got on with reality about as well as blind seagulls get on with jet engines.

Bez's fellow stoner decided that his pal needed some fuel to continue his spontaneous domestic motorbike rally. He picked up a can of petrol which happened to be lying, no doubt to Debs' despair, in the back room. The petrol splashed all over him. He sat down again, contemplated developments, and lit himself a consoling cigarette.

BOOM!!!

BEZ: Yeah, somehow one of me pals ended up with petrol all over him, lit a cig and ended up on fire. I suddenly noticed him running up and down the house, burning all the carpet and shouting, 'PUT ME OUT!'

Then the next thing we knew, we had the fucking fire brigade there, the fucking police, ambulances, the lot, you know. Mind you, it must have been pretty bad, because he ended up in the burns unit for a week.

A week later Bez's pal was out of hospital, Bez's house was still a wreck and Bez had agreed to do the tour.

GAZ: A week went by and we'd almost given up on Bez. Then he called us up and said that he'd changed his mind and he'd do it.

BEZ: It was about a week later that I finally succumbed to money and decided to go for it. And at the time money was the sole reason, because unfortunately in this cruel world of ours, without no money you ain't doing nothing. And I like doing plenty, so it was a means to do plenty.

Meanwhile, back in Manchester, Shaun had also recruited a new member for the band. He'd met Marlon 'Peanut' Vegas, or Nuts, on his fateful summer trip to Ibiza. They'd promised to keep in touch and Shaun wanted him in the new Mondays to dance and maybe do a little rapping and/or singing.

> **SHAUN:** I didn't originally think of Nuts for the Mondays. I wanted him to have a part in *Molly's Idle Ways*. I didn't know which part. I just thought he'd be good. Then we kept in touch after Ibiza, and I said, 'Why don't you join the band?' I thought he'd add a bit of extra stage presence, help Bez along, if Bez decided to do it. It would make us a bit more *New* Happy Mondays.
>
> The Mondays always was a bit of a freak show. It was always a bit of a madhouse on stage. Nuts was just something else just to egg us on, to keep us going. And don't forget Bez is now ten years older than he was, so even he had to have something to make him feel new as well. So Nuts was brought on for that reason as well.

At the request of Simon Moran, Paul Ryder also approached Rowetta, the Mondays backing-singer/soul diva of old.

Rowetta had started singing with the band in 1990 at the request of then manager Nathan McGough. A year earlier, she'd been working as a barmaid in Manchester when Simply Red manager Elliott Rashman heard her singing behind the bar and signed her on the spot. Rowetta had first spoken to Shaun the night before she was due to appear on stage with the Mondays at the 1990 gigs at Manchester's G-Mex.

ROWETTA: The first thing Shaun ever said to me was, 'You might hear I'm a bit of a bastard. Well, I am.'

Rowetta had spent the last six years since the Mondays split bringing up her two children and working with singers like Billy Ocean and Mick Hucknall, as well as teaching singing at a local secondary school. She needed no persuading to come back on board.

ROWETTA: Horse called me up, and said, 'Are you up for the tours?' I'd heard the rumours but hadn't believed it was true. But I said yes. I always got on with them all really good.

Shaun's initial *Sport* column declaration that the Mondays would be re-formed and touring by Christmas was always hopelessly optimistic, but as 1999 dawned, all required parties had signed up for the venture. There remained only one last hurdle. Shaun and Bez, who had gone from being best friends to sworn enemies after the demise of Black Grape, had to formally bury the hatchet.

Nobody knew how this one would go. Everybody was pretty sure, though, that it wouldn't run smoothly – which was how things worked out.

Simon Moran arranged for Shaun, Bez, Paul and Gaz to meet and hammer out their differences at a pub called Jackson's Wharf in the Manchester yuppie dockside residential area of Castle Quays. The pub, with its gothic wooden interior, usually played host to the radio engineers and DJs from local station Key 103 across the quay, or any number of soap stars who live in nearby Castlefield. This evening was to be rather more turbulent than most in that establishment.

Shaun and Bez greeted each other reasonably warmly but warily, like former lovers meeting years later at a family wedding. As the meeting started, however, it quickly became clear that Bez still had reservations. He was still smarting from the original Mondays, when band members had promised him a cut of their PRS payments and then reneged on the deal. Now he had a wife, a family and a home to take care of. He wanted to make sure he could do that. There were financial details to be sorted.

SHAUN: The meeting at Jackson's Wharf was about Bez's payments and what he really wanted. The Mondays would still have re-formed without Bez, but it wouldn't have been as good. We knew that. Simon would still have got the tour together, but the Mondays are a package.

Basically Bez was faffing around over money because in the old Mondays he never got any PRS because he doesn't play an instrument and he doesn't write songs. He still wanted PRS, though. So I donated five per cent from my PRS at this Jackson's Wharf meeting – but then nobody else would budge and give any of theirs. So he ended up just getting some of my cut.

Then we had to resolve the, like, logistics of the tour and how it was going to work. We knew it had to be done in advance. In the past things had got so on top, when there were six of us in the band, that all six people wanted their own tour bus because no one was talking to each other. We'd rent a tour bus, then after a few dates nobody would get on it because I was on it, or Bez was on it. We'd end up with six people all travelling separately having different security which was absolutely fucking ridiculous.

We agreed that we'd all travel together, and our Paul was the funniest at the meeting. He really put his foot down, telling everyone, 'We're not having this and we're not having that,' and laying down the law. Then, on the tour, everyone stuck to the rules apart from one person. Our Paul was the one who ended up wanting first class travel and train tickets for himself and his bird.

But we also agreed at this meeting that if you wanted your woman there you paid for it yourself. It wouldn't come out of the kitty. Then the only person who ended up breaking that was our kid.

And there was one point where things got a bit heated. My mate G-man said something and Bez jumped up and said, 'What do you know? You don't fucking know anything!' And he knocked the table over and beer glasses were flying everywhere.

After that it was alright, though, really.

SIMON MORAN: The meeting at Jackson's Wharf got very heated. Over the years a lot of water had gone under the bridge between Bez and Shaun, and Bez got very angry. Some old wounds got unearthed. It wasn't that pleasant a meeting. It was very nearly violent. Then, somehow, things got agreed.

The concluding meeting took place one week later in the bar of Manchester's Malmaison Hotel, close to Piccadilly station. Bez had chewed over the financial proposal from SJM and the rest of the band proposal and finally agreed to go ahead with things.

Shaun announced this conversion to the world in his *Daily Sport* column in his own inimitable style:

It took us two meetings to persuade Bez. The first one lasted about five hours but the next one was cool. We knocked Bez down from the £50,000 he wanted to £5 and a free Admiral T-shirt. Everyone's finally cool.

And, amazingly, everyone finally *was* cool. All of the band had had initial fears and misgivings about the project, and all had managed to overcome them. Shaun's worry had been that he was now too old for on-the-road life, and he'd also had his vision of band life tainted by the bitter demise of the Mondays and Black Grape. But, of course, he had the taxman to satisfy. He convinced himself it would be different this time.

Paul's worry had been that the band would be reunited only to find that public taste had moved on and they'd be back playing the dreaded Boardwalk. So once he saw a tour itinerary including the MEN Arena and Brixton Academy, he was fine. His only other major fear was getting his smack habit back.

Bez's driving force was solely the financial reward, and SJM and the band had managed to satisfy him on that score. Despite this, he still worried about the Mondays turning into a ludicrous cabaret act. And, as he'd painstakingly explained to Gaz and Horse that mad, ceiling-punching, pyrotechnic night in Glossop, he didn't want to work with fucking junkies.

Gaz Whelan probably had the least misgivings of all the reuniting Mondays. He'd quickly revised his decision to write the music industry out of his life when the comeback tour came along. Now, he just wanted it to be good.

GAZ WHELAN: Of course the money was a factor, and also I really wanted to play one or two big venues again. But when it really came down to it, the money thing was irrelevant. I just wanted a chance for it to be like the old times. I had loads of doubts when we started, but we really wanted it to be not too professional, not too perfect, plenty of space for ad-libbing. We wanted it to be the genuine Mondays article.

BEZ: The Mondays meant everything to me first time around. I would have fought anyone for the band. That's how much it meant to me. This time the motivation initially was totally the money. But I didn't want to spoil the myth. We knew it had to sound good.

To make some money, to bring back the old days, to be like a band again. The Mondays were going into their reunion tour with heady objectives. This could turn out to be a glorious triumph or a hideous narcotic disaster. Or maybe both. It was time for Happy Mondays, for the first time in six years, to go back into a recording studio together.

4. MANIC MONDAYS IN STUDIO MAYHEM

Tiny studio has view of car park, Rowetta mistakes river for path, Shaun unable to get out of bed, PD brands Shaun 'a penis', G-man accidentally robs band, lobster enters Shaun's pants.

It was finally decided that the new Mondays tour would begin towards the end of April 1999, with European dates and other festivals to be added as time went on. As it stood now the line-up was Shaun, Rowetta and Nuts on vocals, Bez dancing, Paul Ryder on bass, Gaz Whelan on drums, Wags on guitar, and Ben Leach on keyboards and acting as musical director. Neil Mather, a freelance tour manager working under the SJM umbrella, was made, er, tour manager.

The final meeting was held in the first week of February 1999, leaving just over two months until the first date, a warm-up gig at Hereford, on April 21. As soon as everyone was agreed and everything was definitely going ahead practice rooms were booked at the Greenhouse rehearsal rooms, in Stockport.

The lynchpin on the production side of things was Ben Leach. Liverpool-born Ben has the classic Scouser look – short hair, sporty clothes, and if you didn't know him you wouldn't leave your bag in the same room as him. Stereotypes aside, Ben began his music career as a classically trained trumpet player in the brass section of Scouse rockers The Farm. Coming from a musical family Ben had also learned to play the piano as a kid and when the band sacked the brass

section he slyly wangled his way on to keyboards. As
he explains: 'Mum was a piano teacher, and I wasn't
allowed to go out and play footie with me mates. It
was "you're going to learn the piano", and I fucking
hated it, but at the end of the day I got a job out of it.'
Since the split of The Farm in 1994 Ben had worked
freelance as a keyboard programmer and technician for
everyone from the Lighthouse Family to Status Quo
and the Brand New Heavies.

Promoter Simon Moran had known Ben from when
he used to promote The Farm, and approached him at
a James gig at Wembley in December 1998, with the
proposition to come and work with the Mondays.

BEN LEACH: I met Simon Moran backstage at a
James gig. I wasn't working there or anything, I
was just ligging, getting some free booze out of the
dressing room and all that. And there I was in the
production office, happily drinking away and
Simon Moran came in and said, 'I'm thinking
about getting the Mondays together, are you up
for it?' or words to that effect – and I said yes. I
didn't hear anything more for ages, but finally I
got a call and went to meet them all for the first
time, at the Malmaison meeting.

It had been a long time since any of the Mondays had
been in a studio/rehearsal room environment. The once
familiar surroundings of walls carpeted to dampen the
sound, wedge monitors, mike-stands and mixing desks,
a multi-coloured fag-ash and beer-can bolognese of
spaghetti leads across the floor and the gaping hollow
recesses of the bass bins were all strangers to them

now. And just as strange to them were the songs they had written together about ten years ago. The ravages of time and chemicals had taken their toll on memory. It was going to be a total relearning process for the Mondays, or more like a serious cramming session. They only had two months to remember how to play their songs before they were expected up on stage at the Manchester Evening News Arena in front of 16,000 people and the world's press. Piece of piss!

It was Ben's job as musical director to rehearse the band and basically teach them how to play their own songs again. Which meant first having to learn the songs, tunes and all the various parts for himself.

Shaun and the others had already made it clear they wanted to do the original songs with a new twist to them. They wanted it heavy and they wanted it dance-style, more like the Oakenfold and Wetherall remixes; they needed to be reinvented a bit to bring them up to date and give them a new edge. So for the three weeks prior to the initial meeting Ben had been trying to track down the master tapes of the Mondays' early recordings to work from. These were the master copies of everything from 'Delightful', the first ever single, to *Pills 'N' Thrills*. There should have been over 130 reels of tape. But despite all efforts, Ben only managed to track down a handful.

The masters were meant to be the raw material from which the Mondays' songs were to be reborn in their new, fuller-sounding forms. But without any of the masters, which split the songs into their component parts, Ben would have to work from the actual albums, taking samples and guidance from them.

BEN: I tried to get the masters but they had all been lost. Theoretically they belong to Factory which doesn't exist any more so they should have reverted to London Records, but nobody could find them. I think out of 130-odd master tapes they could find four reels and there was nothing on them. They were useless.

I found a box of computer disks which had a few bits and bobs from the original stuff. There were hundreds of them, but only about two that were useful. The rest were all shite. There were a few of Rowetta's vocals and a couple of drum loops. Oakenfold and Osborne also gave me a few DATs, but it was mainly all remixed stuff which wasn't very useful as we were trying to re-create the original versions. Shaun wanted to make it a bit different, but still keep some of the original elements.

In the end I actually had to resample from the records, so I got the CDs and just cobbled it together from there. Luckily I already had most of them, being a bit of a fan.

As rock'n'roll history in Manchester goes, the Greenhouse recording studio has seen it, done it, picked what was left up off the floor when the bands had gone home for the night and smoked it. It is a converted warehouse on an industrial estate behind an Office World superstore. It's situated at the end of an unsurfaced track with more potholes in it than Cheddar Gorge, with a concrete ramp leading up to the front door. A battered old intercom is stuck to the wall, and inside two flights of steel stairs lead up to an office and the seven rehearsal rooms, which have been hired by everyone from Oasis to Cleopatra.

For the first three weeks the Mondays were put into Showcase Two, a tiny sound-proofed room costing only £50 a day for hire. It's about 10ft by 20ft with green carpet on three walls and the ceiling. The fourth wall has a window with a wonderful view across the car park.

The first rehearsal took place on Monday 15 February 1999, just eight and a half weeks before the Hereford date. Wags, Gaz Whelan and Paul Ryder arrived at the Greenhouse just after 10 a.m. For the last two years Gaz's drum-kit had lain under the stairs at his Swinton home doing little else apart from gathering dust. Paul's bass had been propped against the wall in Worsley. Now, at long last, they were back in action.

It was strange and slightly ominous that almost exactly ten years earlier the arrival of acid house and the start of the whole Madchester scene was marked by a *Top Of The Pops* appearance featuring both the Mondays and The Stone Roses in November 1989. Now, ten years down the line, what was left of the Mondays and The Stone Roses' Ian Brown found themselves rehearsing next door to each other at the Greenhouse. Ian was preparing to tour his solo material and the Mondays were getting ready to do their thing.

BEN LEACH: It was like a prison sentence. We got stuck in there because it was cheap. It was basically just used like a little programming room, because we weren't having everyone at the same time. In the daytime I'd record the band on to tape, then they would leave and Shaun, Rowetta and Nuts would arrive in the evening.

Rehearsals lasted anything from eight to twelve hours a day, and there were political reasons for keeping the singers separate from the musicians. Simon Moran thought the only way of making sure things got as far as the first gig was to keep Paul and Shaun away from each other as much as possible. The relationship between the brothers is unfathomable, except to say that when they fall out they do it in glorious style and no one knows when it's going to happen – or why. Not even themselves. As Paul Ryder puts it: 'Just brothers being brothers, innit? You know, I don't even know what it's about.' Long-time pal of the pair Nigel Pivaro, aka Terry Duckworth from *Coronation Street*, says the brothers have opposite personalities; Paul is the sober Yin to Shaun's raging Yang. Or something like that.

NIGEL PIVARO: Shaun is the oldest so he's the extrovert, and Paul is the sensitive one. He's shyer than Shaun and more aware of his responsibilities. Shaun is more dynamic and outgoing, but to the same degree can be a bit of a loose cannon at times . . .

There were still a few doubts that first morning. The combination of warring brothers, old hands and new faces Ben and Wags made all the ingredients for a tense stand-off. But thankfully it never materialised; maturity and experience had tempered the burning passions and spirits which led to so many rehearsal-room rucks in the early days.

Ben stood behind his banks of keyboards and recording equipment. Gaz was at the back of the room, Paul to his right and Wags to his left. It had been Mark Day's funk-pop *wah-wah* guitar which characterised the sound of the band in the early days. Now it was up to Wags to bring the old songs alive again. And he did this with aplomb.

Paul Wagstaff cures hangovers with half a pint of brandy. He is 100 per cent old-school rock star; straight from the Shaun Ryder finishing school of excellence in excess which teaches you how to keep a note in your nose, a fag in your mouth and a large measure of spirit in your hand. Sounds easy? Try it! The fact that he played a mean guitar was a bonus and it soon became clear that no one would be missing Mark Day.

GAZ WHELAN: It seemed like it hadn't been six years since we'd played, it seemed like it had been six months. You'd think it would be a bit awkward for at least the first couple of rehearsals. But it wasn't, even for the first couple of minutes; it just fuckin' fell back into place straight away.

There was no problem with the new faces. I thought Wags' guitar-playing was great. If the band could have been hand-picked and put together in the first place then Wags would have been on guitar from day one, he really fitted in and after a week it was like he'd always been there. I love Wags' stuff, I love the way he ad-libs and fucks up.

I would actually have liked PD to have been there doing his thing, because he plays different things every night and adds new things to the music which I really like. But there was no chance of that happening, and sometimes you need someone who's got a really high-tech computer brain, like Ben had, in case anything fucks up.

And what, indeed, had the two absent members been doing since the demise of the Mondays? Of Mark Day the band members had heard little. Cowhead had played for a short while with Davis, Gaz Whelan and Andy Rourke in Delicious, then tried some stuff with 808 State and then finally quit the music business for good, taking a job and dedicating himself to raising his kids with his estate agent wife, Jane.

Paul 'PD' Davis had worked on various music projects with little success, and was rumoured to be still extremely bitter about the break-up. After the Mondays' split he penned a book which numerous publishers refused to publish because of its allegedly extremely libellous content. So what did the two outsiders make of the Ryders' return? Did they wish their old colleagues well?

I tracked Moose and PD down while the Mondays were in Greenhouse and found them in less-than-forgiving mood.

MOOSE: I knew that I would never get asked to rejoin the band 'cos me and Shaun didn't get on. I mean, really, I think it's farcical. What must the punters think? We were always supposed to be a cool band. I don't care what the band say, they're all doing it for the money. They're all hypocrites, the lot of them.

Do I miss the band? Well, I miss the banter. But the band weren't really my mates. Shaun screwed me up. He walked away from a £2 million pound deal we were about to sign. That was the end of the Mondays. Of course I was fed up. Sorry Shaun, but no, I don't give anyone a second chance like that, even though you've had tons of them. Who can want a Kentucky Fried Chicken that much?

I think Shaun's an animal. He's a nutcase. I wouldn't trust him an inch. There are a lot of nasty things I could say about him, which I won't. I'm sure PD will do, though.

When I do something I do it to the best of my ability and I put a lot of effort into it. Shaun's the opposite. He does as little as possible and makes excuses. For fifteen years I used to just shrug and say, 'Oh that's Shaun.' But how many times are you supposed to say, 'Oh that's Shaun'?

I'm not just saying this because I'm jealous that I'm not involved. I've left the music business. I got messed about with and I've had enough of all that. I've got a straight job now. I just picked the paper up one day and saw a job selling books door-to-door. I love it. Well, I don't love it, but I only do four or five hours each day, and it pays my mortgage. You can't be in a band until you're 60, can you? You'll end up like the stuff you read in the papers – perverts and Gary Glitters and that one out of The Bay City Rollers.

I've got two children now, Jasmine and Cameron, I love them dearly, I love playing with

them, I love being there when they come home.
There's still an element of frustration, but you
have to live with that. I'm grateful that I'm not
caught up in a circus, unlike a few people I know.

I've got mixed feelings, though. I still get PRS,
so I want the Mondays to go on tour and promote
the back catalogue. It's good for me!

PD: I wasn't really aware of what was going on
behind my back in '93. I wasn't enjoying what I
was doing for the last couple of years of it. Shaun
is just a penis. You know when I look at the band
now, I'm totally aware of why I left. Well, you
don't step in dog shit twice with sandals on, do
yer? It's never impressed me, any band getting
back together whatever the situation, but it's easy
to say when you didn't do it I suppose. I was there
first time round.

I've learned the hard way, and they should have
too, and yet they've been sucked back into this
fucking nightmare of underpaid fucking children
wages, with all those hangers-on, all those fucking
suckers, all those fucking sly friends, all these
management and agents and bullshitters. You
don't fucking need 'em. Everybody who I ever met
who dealt with Happy Mondays were
abcess-fucking-eating maggots.

I've got nothing but admiration for the band
when I was in them and then nothing but horror
for them afterwards. But basically I don't give a
fuck, I made a supreme choice in '93 and everyone
who went back on to that fucking bandwagon,
surrounded by the Indians and the bandits, got

fucking scalped again. I didn't and I'm so fucking proud of that.

What would I have said if I'd been asked to rejoin? I would possibly have said, 'Smoke my fucking arse hairs.'

Paul Davis is single, and has no children. He currently lives in south Manchester and is working with Rowetta on a dance track. He is also trying to get a break into acting, in a film called *Social Soup* based in Manchester.

For a lot of people Moose and PD were the sound of the Mondays, the swirling scally-funk backdrop to Ryder's pulp-suburbia ramblings. And if there are such things as Mondays purists – concerned with the music rather than the quality of their pills – then they probably missed them too.

Neither have forgiven and neither have forgotten. In fact it's probably a safe bet to state that neither Cowhead nor PD have been able to stomach a Kentucky Fried Chicken since 1993.

Meanwhile, back in the recording studio, G-man had been employed by Shaun as his PA. This meant it was G-man's job to look after Shaun's immediate interests. This role was to be short-lived, and came to a very sticky end.

Whilst the band were brushing up their old material, Simon Moran had thrashed out a deal with London Records for a single to be recorded, and for a reworked *Greatest Hits* album to be released. The chosen song was Thin Lizzy's 'The Boys Are Back In Town'. This was a fitting tribute to one of rock'n'roll's most notorious gangs.

'The Boys Are Back . . .' seemed the perfect song to herald their return. The original lyrics, penned by the late Phil Lynott, were about a bunch of hell-raisers whose laddish antics made them famous. It sounded pretty much spot-on for the Mondays.

PAUL RYDER: When the tour was finalised, I said to Gaz, 'Fucking hell, it would be a good idea to walk on stage while Thin Lizzy's "The Boys Are Back in Town" is playing.' Anyway, weeks later we were all on our way down to London in a Space Cruiser to do the first lot of press for the tour. Suddenly, our kid turned round and said, "I've got a good idea for a single, we'll do 'The Boys Are Back In Town' " and me and Gaz said, "Fucking hell, no way!", cos we'd been talking about it. I'd actually just been out and bought Thin Lizzy's *Live and Dangerous* on CD because I hadn't had it since I was at school. And as Shaun said it I just went "Here y'are, I've brought it with me!". It felt like everyone starting to think along the same lines again. It was also a natural choice for Oakenfold and Osborne to produce, seeing as they'd produced *Pills 'N' Thrills*.

Through a mutual friend Shaun approached Lynott's mother Phyllis Lynott, in Ireland and asked for permission to re-record the song and re-write the lyrics for a Mondays version. She gave him her blessing and London Records sorted out the legal details so the recording could go ahead. Then, after three weeks in the tiny shoebox of a rehearsal room at the Greenhouse, the band were treated to a radical change of scenery – they were sent to one of Britain's plushest residential recording studious: Hookend Manor, in rural Oxfordshire. It was here that they were to record the new single. Oakey and Osborne were brought in to help, and altogether the band spent a week in the 25-acre grounds of the £1,000-a-day studio putting it together.

The reasoning, as with every other studio the Mondays have been to, was to put them somewhere nice, but out of the way from any drugs scene. It's a line of reasoning that has caused more trouble than it has ever prevented, with Barbados as the textbook example. This is because if anyone wants drugs, they simply take them with them.

This journey saw Shaun and his new PA, G-man, carting shitloads of downers with them to the studios. This was because in a studio, ninety-nine per cent of the time is spent aiting. And waiting time is usually spent either getting bored, getting fit if there's an on-site gym, or getting off your trolley. No prizes for guessing which one got the most votes from Shaun and G-man.

And so it was that for the first three days Shaun refused to get out of bed to add any vocals, telling the producers to get Rowetta to put hers down first and he would do his then. Messengers were dispatched with Mercurian speed to find and bring Rowetta down to the studios from her Manchester home.

ROWETTA: I was supposed to go down on a Wednesday or a Thursday, with Nuts. Then I got a call saying could I come down a couple of days earlier because Shaun wouldn't get out of bed.

Shaun kept saying, 'Get Row to sing something first,' so I did. He'd had a lot of sleeping tablets.

Things then started to go a lot more smoothly. That was until G-man got off his tits and tried to rob the place.

First things first: G-man is not a thief. Not normally. This was most definitely the exception rather than the rule. What basically happened is he got so completely shredded he went off on a wild one-man mission one night and took hostage a cash box that was lying around in Oakey's room, while everyone else was in the studio downstairs.

Now, G-man is a lovely man with a lovely girlfriend and a lovely daughter. And when he woke up the next day he was as gobsmacked as everyone else and couldn't believe what he had done.

Of course he gave the cash back straight away and apologised profusely, but there was no way he could carry on working on the tour now and, sadly, he left for Manchester on the next train.

SHAUN: What happened was G-man got off his bollocks. He was there working for me, and the man got right off his head.

He got a load of valium, a load of diazepam and a load of temazepam and he ate the bloody lot. He ate all mine as well, didn't know where he was. He thought he was someone else, somewhere else and he robbed the place.

Everyone else was pissed off with him because they thought it was disrespectful to me. But he's a loyal worker, he just lost it a bit, like everyone does now and then. He has been forgiven by Simon Moran now, but it ruined him being able to work with rest of us, otherwise he would still be on the firm now.

After G-man's unfortunate departure, recording continued until all the tracks for the single were down. The next weekend would be spent at yet another studio, Peter Gabriel's Real World in Wiltshire.

Gabriel's Real World is a dog's bollocks sort of studio. The building started off life as a water-mill in the 1700s, and has had several incarnations since then, including a short spell as a girls' school. Now it sits as though on an island between a duck pond and a running stream known as the By Brook, in Corsham, near Bath.

The location is now a real hippy paradise, surrounded as it is by leylines and ancient burial grounds. It is built over the running water itself, and can either set your creative juices flowing by flicking your switch, or your gastric juices flowing by making you sea-sick. Glass panels in the floor let you see through to the flowing water beneath your feet. Which is nice ... if you like brown flowing water.

The only real problem with Real World, as with any place which features lots of water and bridges, is trying to navigate your way around it in the dark. It seems that for either aesthetic or deeply sadistic purposes, the designers decided not to erect safety-rails along the paths which take you from the studio to the various cottages and other amenities which lie on dry land. Instead they leave it up to the highly responsible individuals working there to be sensible enough to remember where they are going. A good honest formula for developing those character-building orienteering skills and bringing out true leadership qualities, but a real bastard bad idea if you're half-cut on Bushmills whisky and suddenly realise you've left your fags on the other side of the pond. As Rowetta found out one night.

ROWETTA: We had some interviews lined up. Shaun and Bez and Nuts came really late, so I had to go and do them. I don't like doing interviews when I'm drunk, because I say things I shouldn't say. And when Shaun and Bez came, we carried it on over dinner. I was extremely drunk, but they reported all of what I said. I think it was for *Time Out* and I was going on about Shaun's penis. Then there was a photoshoot where Shaun had a lobster down his pants and he was dead embarrassed afterwards in case the picture might get out.

Anyway, I'd left my cigs in one of the places where we'd had the photos done, so I had to go back to get them from this hut on the other side of the water. I stepped on to what I thought was a shiny path but was actually shiny water. All of a sudden I realised the water was right up to my nose. I had to tip-toe to keep my head above the water. I couldn't get out. So I just stood there, pissed.

Eventually someone helped me out and then I had to hide from the photographers. I was covered in duck shit. Steve Osborne said later that he'd

had visions of me floating along under the studio
floor banging on the glass . . .

The single was released on 10 April 1999. It kicked off
with a waxy guitar riff and an honest salutation from
Shaun, singing 'Guess who's back for your money . . .'
It included 'Lazyitis', 'Bob's Yer Uncle' and 'Loose Fit'
as extra tracks. However, despite these old favourites,
it only sold around 35,000 copies, going into the charts
at Number 24.

Two weeks later, when the tour was in full swing,
the reworked *Greatest Hits* album was released and hit
the Number Eleven spot, selling over 100,000 copies.

The first airplay 'The Boys Are Back' got was on
Steve Lamacq's show in late March '99. He managed
to get his hands on the only copy of the song, taken
straight from the master to a writeable CD. He played
it while Fatboy Slim was a guest in the studio and then
nicked it from the station to play during one of his
guest DJ-ing spots at Birmingham the following
weekend.

STEVE LAMACQ: I thought it was a good choice,
though they could have made more of the chorus.

My show's producer at the time, Rhys Jones,
made it quite clear to London Records that he
wanted it first. He was a Mondays fan from the
first time around. He said 'Look, we've got to
have this Mondays record first; we've done the
interview and everything so just give us the single
and that'll be fine thank you very much, no
arguments about it.' So it came in and we played
it. Then I nicked the only copy that there was in

existence and played it at The Sanctuary on Saturday night!

FATBOY SLIM: I really liked it, but I couldn't see how it was a cover of a Thin Lizzy song. When Steve Lamacq played it I was like, 'Hey this is good, what's this?' and he said it was the new Mondays track, and that it was a cover of 'The Boys Are Back'. I'm thinking, No it's not, but it's very good!

Fatboy Slim, aka Norman Cook, had been mooted by SJM as a possible contender for remixing a Mondays track for release instead of the single. A message had come to Shaun via SJM that Norman wanted a hand-written letter asking him to do it, because he thought it was some sort of wind-up. So Shaun penned a note asking Norman to do a remix of the classic baggy anthem 'Kinky Afro', and sent it to him in the States.

FATBOY SLIM: I got a fax from Shaun when I was in America. It was handwritten which is quite nice as these things usually come through record companies. It said, 'Can you phone me at me mum's house.'

There had been talk about me remixing one of his tracks, but when something was that good in the first place I don't like messing with it. Unless I've really got an idea how to make them better it's really hard to work on a track you like and you know really well, because you feel like they've already been done.

TONY WILSON: We said at Factory, we would have gone back and done a really super remix of '24 Hour Party People', which always deserved something special doing to it. That would have been a better idea.

BEZ: The new single was all right, but personally I would have done a new track. A brand new Mondays tune. It was nothing to do with me; I was just along for the ride and had no say in the tune whatsoever. It was other people's shouts.

And at the end of the day it was someone else's tune. Some nights I could get into it, some nights I couldn't.

JO WHILEY: It's not my favourite single they've ever done to be honest. I wasn't wildly into it. I wasn't expecting them to put one out so soon, I think that was part of the problem. Maybe they rushed it a bit too much.

MOOSE: Oh dear, I heard that one. I thought it was shit. It just makes me cringe. Doing 'The Boys Are Back'? Thin Lizzy? That's just ruined that one, you know what I mean, I thought that was an excellent Thin Lizzy track and I wouldn't have attempted to do it. And the way they did it . . . oh, it's the usual shit, innit?

SIMON MORAN: I just did the deal for the single, it was up to them what they did artistically. I don't think it was very good to be honest with you. You know, it would be great to see them make a great record, which I think they can do, but that wasn't it.

ROWETTA: I thought it was a joke at first. Then I heard what they were doing and it sounded really, really good. I heard Wags for the first time then and I thought he was great, the things he was doing on guitar.

Meanwhile the Mondays had returned to a punishing rehearsal schedule back at the Greenhouse, though this time in the much plusher surroundings of Showcase One. This studio was five times bigger than Showcase Two, with a full PA rig. From 5 April, they were rehearsing for the tour as a whole, with Shaun, Rowetta and Nuts singing and percussionist Lee Mullen brought in to add another dimension to the live sound.

By now sixteen tunes in total had been rehearsed including the old favourite '24 Hour Party People', from a wish-list of songs put together by Gaz, Paul, Ben, Shaun and Simon Moran. These were finally whittled down to around twelve for the set-list, which in the final weeks before the tour began were run through again and again and again. Rehearsals went well, too. Shaun broke up the tedium with impromptu Elvis impressions, and made the rest of the band follow him on their instruments as he launched into regular outbursts of 'Suspicious Minds' while performing a Presley-style leg wobble for added effect. He would occasionally stop all work to regale the rest of the band with anecdotes of old times and ex members of the band. Once Shaun urged the others on in typical style:

'Look, I've had two grams of charlie and I've only had two brandies; I need something more to drink before I can get into it. You guys get your arses in gear and play and I'll be right with you.'

Shaun had forgotten the lyrics to most of the songs he had written years before, so everything was written down on pieces of paper. These were pinned to walls, mike stands and speakers, or taped to the floor so he could see them and sing them. When the tour began they were all input into a PC and fed to an autocue on the stage. He didn't need them after the first few weeks, but left them there anyway.

Rehearsals went on, and on, and on. It was more work than they had ever put into a show in the history of the Mondays. But in the heady days of acid house, the Mondays weren't about massive effort and perfection. They were about fun, anarchy and laughing all the way to the cemetery – via the bank. This time, though, they had something to prove. If it was going to work it was going to have to be good.

GAZ WHELAN: Rehearsals went really, really well. We changed a few things, sat down, listened to them and changed them again to make them live and then about four weeks after learning the songs and the tunes, Shaun came in and did his singing straight away. I hadn't heard from Shaun for six years, you know, never mind played in a band with him, but when he started singing it sent shivers down my spine. It all came together. It was really weird.

We used bits from the remixes and the loops to make it a bit heavier and groovier. I was really,

really fucking pleased with the way everything sounded in the end. When we started I thought it would be pretty good, but I didn't think it would be *that* good. By the time we were fully rehearsing all the songs and X was singing and everything I was pretty surprised how good it was. I think it sounded better than it did before. Everyone was a lot more professional about it this time. It was more practice than we've ever done and harder practice than we'd ever done. I think everyone was determined not to make cunts of themselves.

We had been rehearsing for about two weeks and I think we had got about five or six songs together, and Bez came in halfway through. We were playing, and he sat down and started nodding his head. You always know when you're doing new tunes whether Bez likes them or not because he'd do his thing a little bit. He looked at me and said, 'Fucking hell, it sounds better than ever!'

Various visitors called into the Greenhouse to see the band rehearsing, including long-time Mondays fan and boxer Prince Naseem, who popped in to say hello the night before a bout at the Manchester Evening News Arena. And true to form, throughout the period of the band's stay the off-licence round the corner from the practice rooms had to buy in extra stocks of Bushmills whisky, Benson & Hedges and Stella Artois to keep the party in Showcase One up and running.

While everyone else was practising playing and singing, Bez was doing his own preparation. He was conducting meticulous research to find the right sort of stick to wave about on stage. 'The Boys Are Back . . .' had given him a singing role for the first time. Well, not a singing role exactly, but he got to say *'I be voodoo,'* a few times at the end of the song and he did it really menacingly. And if Bez was going to act voodoo, he was going to damn well look voodoo, too. So he bought a voodoo book to find out just what sort of stick voodoo men are supposed to have. It turned out to be one with a skull on the top. Eventually, several people gave him presents of sticks with real skulls on the top, including the artist Damien Hirst. The one Shaun's holding on the cover of this book was one of the ones Rowetta got him, but which never got used on stage. (Some people have said at first glance at the book cover, they thought it was a picture of Shaun and Bez.)

In the end Rowetta got him the stick he wanted. It was a black cane topped with a small golden skull and he used it for the massive Manchester show.

Stage show aside, no one gives a fuck what the Mondays look like. Even in their heyday they were no oil paintings. But what they have always had is attitude. And that comes out through the music, the lyrics and through the spectacle that is Bez. And there was a whole new generation of fans this time around, who were coming to see just what they'd missed out on first time around.

STEVE LAMACQ: There was huge demand amongst the younger generation, a generation who'd never seen the Mondays. From people who actually desperately wanted to see them, because they were so bored of their older brothers telling them what they'd missed out on.

Originally the Mondays were on the crest of a breaking wave. They could never do that again, but they certainly have a place in club culture which meant that they were never going to be out of touch. And as much as they kept saying 'We're only doing this for the money,' I think it was a valid thing for them to do. In general, I hate bands re-forming. I hated all the punk bands I liked as a kid getting back together, whereas I think the Mondays still had a sort of relevance.

Finally, on Friday 16 April 1999, with one new single and eight weeks of practice under their Adidas belts, the Happy Mondays checked out of the Greenhouse. They had got through 34 plectrums, six drum skins, two sets of bass strings, two sets of guitar strings, 54 Elastoplast, eight drum sticks, eight batteries, four reels of tape, 6,440 cigarettes, 32 bottles of whisky, 448 cans of Stella, 174 cans of diet coke, 112 pies, 50 portions of chips (35 with a roll), three human skulls and various quantities of chemicals and hashish since they started rehearsing, eight weeks before. Now it was time to have some fun.

5. DRUG BAND IN TOUR TRIUMPH

Band spend £2,000 on porn, author slaps out fire in socks, Bez's puke 'looks like tar', Mondays tout their own gig, Schmeichel forced to view underpants, King Dong hits the headlines, human skull thrown to crowd, Shaun shoots Ali G, band ponder white dog shit, and Shaun seen to dance on stage. Allegedly.

Happy Mondays Live on Tour 1999

April

21	Hereford Leisure Centre
23	Manchester Evening News Arena
24/25	Glasgow SECC
27/28/29	London, Brixton Academy

May

1	Dublin, SFX Club

June

14	Ibiza, Manumission

July

6	Norway, Quart Festival
10	Galway, Ireland
11	Edinburgh, T In The Park

August

2	Japan, The Mount Fuji Rock Festival
6	Portugal, The Sudoeste Festival
11	Cornwall, the Eclipse Festival
21/22	Leeds/Chelmsford, V99
28	Dublin, Slane Castle

Next, of course, was the tour. For months the band had been talking the talk, now it was time to walk the walk. The prospect of the Mondays coming back on the road was more talked about even than the Sex Pistols' second coming, which had taken place a year earlier and left everyone with a foul taste in their mouths. The Great Rock'n'Roll Swindle wouldn't work twice. There was a back-breaking weight of expectation upon Shaun and the gang, not only from the press, but from the fans. But if anyone was feeling that weight they kept it well hidden.

For some inexplicable reason the first gig was to be held at Hereford Leisure Centre. It was supposed be a warm-up, and someone at SJM had the idea that it would be great to do a warm-up in the back-arse of beyond. That way, if it was crap, not that many people would hear about it.

But in a case of the ridiculous to the sublime, the next date was in Manchester for a homecoming gig at the 18,000 capacity Manchester Evening News Arena (formerly Nynex). This was the real start of the tour, and an unfulfilled ambition of Bez's who had regretted never having played there (even though it wasn't actually built during the band's first incarnation). Expectations were at their highest for this massive gig in the Mondays' own home town.

Following Manchester there would be a trip up to Glasgow where two nights at the 8,000-capacity SECC had already sold out, before the band were to head back down to London for three nights at the Brixton Academy. The final gig of the official tour was to be at the SFX club in Dublin, which, despite having the best rider of all the venues, was a grotty hole in the rough

Northside area of the city, and a scary prospect. Other dates before the end of the year would also see the band making appearances at V99, Edinburgh's T In The Park, the Mount Fuji Festival in Japan, Norway and, of course, the opening party of the superclub Manumission in Ibiza.

Before the tour began, the band travelled to London to do some press. Bez and Shaun appeared on the covers of the nation's most prestigious music mags. Even the new frothy showbiz gossip paper *Heat* ran a spread on them. The music press was brimming with excitement.

That trip to London was the Mondays' first meeting with the press as a band for six years. They travelled down on a Friday, with Shaun and Bez appearing on Channel Four's *TFI Friday*, meeting various muso hacks over the course of the weekend, and doing an interview for Radio One's Steve Lamacq on Saturday night. It was the first interview Bez had given since the Mondays split, and he needed a lot of reassurance from Radio One that he wasn't going to be done up like a kipper again. It was also to be 25-year-old Nuts' first taste of doing press and interviews.

STEVE LAMACQ: Shaun was very tired – I think he'd been at *TFI* the previous day and he'd had a night out in London as well. I always used to think when I was a young *NME* journalist and the Mondays were first happening that he was rather scary, but he's actually very easy to get along with. Bez was fine, too, once I'd explained what the deal was; I told him, 'This is just going to be an interview and it's not in any way, shape or form some sort of stitch-up. It's just you giving information to our listeners about the Mondays being back together. Tell the story like you want to tell it.'

Nuts was a bit like a youth team player who'd been called to the first team and scored on his debut. He was still obviously just a lad who wasn't in the pop music industry and didn't know how it worked. But the look on his face was one of being a bit taken aback – kind of, 'People are interested in me, as well!' which was quite sweet. You imagine there's more arrogance involved with the Mondays than there actually is when you get to talk to them.

It was April 1999, and for the last week before the tour began, the band were sound-checking and running through the set again and again in the main arena at the Birmingham NEC. It was a long way from the Greenhouse in Stockport, Manchester where they had been practising since February. As well as getting them used to big venues again, the NEC days were fine-tuning the band's ability to work together on stage. During this few days at the NEC they also recorded a special set for Radio One DJ Annie Nightingale's *Thirty Years On Radio* which was to be broadcast on-air during a live party. Shaun and Annie go back a long way and he had wanted to go and play there in person, but the party was the same date as the first Glasgow gig, so they made a recording at the NEC, stuck it on a CD and sent it down to the London studios.

While this was going on they had been staying at Birmingham's Copthorne Hotel while everything was sorted out for the tour. The band kept a low profile, spending days at the NEC and the evenings in their rooms or maybe popping into the bar downstairs.

The anticipation everywhere was reaching fever point, but unusually for the gang, the night before the Hereford gig was spent calmly sat in the hotel bar where the conversation was about times past and Manchester United's chances of the treble. The most noise came from a gang of sales reps across the other side of the room. Shaun was nowhere to be seen. Rowetta was collecting her costume which had been tailor-made for her, along with some cheerleader pom-poms. Eventually the others decided to go out and get something to eat.

Bez, Wags and Nuts went to a Japanese restaurant not far from the hotel. They only wanted a quiet meal, but were soon reminded that their recently re-won fame had its price.

The whole thing started off when a woman, about 23 with brunette hair, approached the table. She introduced herself and her boyfriend, both of them obviously wankered on too much Sapporo and Saki, and insisted on sitting with the boys whilst the food was served. She then began to make her intentions towards Bez clear by dropping hints which were about as subtle as a dayglo orange anorak. When a vendor came in selling red roses she paid £1 for one and handed it over the table to Bez while winking and licking her lips, in a way that should only really happen in Benny Hill sketches.

Obviously her poor boyfriend was less than happy at the way the evening was unfolding. He retaliated by purchasing the remains of the rose-seller's bucket and handing them to his girlfriend in a touching gesture of his devotion. She of course handed the lot over to Bez at which point her man-friend announced it was time to go and they should get their coats.

'Thank fuck for that,' said Bez as they left, not wanting anything to do with any groupies. But the woman was not to be got rid of so easily. Two minutes later she staggered in the door once again.

'I left him down the road, I told him he's boring,' she announced to a roomful of diners by now perplexed, annoyed and intrigued in equal measures. As she spoke, her other half appeared behind her once more, took her by the arm and they were gone. Again.

This time it was a good five minutes before she re-entered again.

'I've definitely lost him now.'

'What?' said Bez.

'I've definitely lost him, I doubled back on myself and he's gone for good this time. I hope you're worth it, you bastard.'

'Look, love, I'm very flattered, but I'm not interested. You've got the wrong end of the stick,' said Bez.

'Listen, get me a drink, and I'll be back in a minute' she replied, oblivious to Bez's attempts to fend her off. 'I'm just off to the loo.'

As soon as she was gone the lads stood up, grabbed their coats, threw some cash on to the table and made a beeline back to the Copthorne.

When the tour bus arrived the next day everyone checked out of the hotel and hopped on. It was a great big bugger with fourteen beds, a lounge area and a fridge full of Stella Artois. This was it then. Next stop Hereford, a town famous as the training home of the

SAS and, er, that's it really. Other great luminaries of the showbiz world who had graced the same boards of Hereford Leisure Centre included the hamster-eating Freddie Starr and a Russian roller-skating troupe who performed *Snow White*. Follow that, then.

It was finally starting to seem real. Back in November the reunion tour had seemed a bit of a pipe dream (there were certainly pipes involved at the time, anyway), but here we finally were, on board the tourbus heading down the motorway to the first venue. Admittedly it wasn't an amazing venue, but it would do. It would be good to see the crowd's reaction, and good to see the band back on stage where they belonged.

As we travelled, tour manager Neil went through the band's hotel bills from Birmingham and worked out that an incredible £2,000 had been spent purely on subscriptions to the porn channels. I told the newsdesk at the *Daily Sport*, who got quite excited at their first scoop of the tour and asked me to file it a.s.a.p., which I did.

Shaun hadn't shown his face until that morning. It soon became clear he was suffering from a real case of nerves. He had been having tranquillisers brought down from Manchester and during the rehearsals at the NEC he had ended up in a real state.

NEIL MATHER: Basically we had to spend extra money to rehearse the full production in a big arena so that they could see what it looked like, and everyone gained a bit of confidence from it. We'd been there for two days and we were due to load out at 5 p.m. I'd had people running up and down the motorway getting Shaun his tablets for him because he was a fucking wreck. And if you'd asked me at 3 p.m. when I was driving us down to do this session, if the tour would have happened I would have said, 'no fucking way'.

Shaun was so off it he wanted the remote control for the TV in the transit van I was driving. This would have been fine if only there was a TV in there. He didn't know what day it was or anything. When we got there he was sat in this room and said the walls and chairs were talking at him. He'd just worked himself into such a frenzy.

Then he went out on stage between 4 p.m. and 5 p.m. on the final day, did one take of the set for Annie Nightingale's Radio One show and it was fucking brilliant. The whole thing was done in one go. It was the first time he'd sung on a stage for years, he was feeling like shit and his pills had only just kicked in, but it was absolutely really fucking brilliant. Shaun was absolutely shitting it, but when he finally came out he really did the business. I think we were all gobsmacked.

ROWETTA: He was nervous all the way through it. He turned up at rehearsals most days, but he was a mess. I told Neil to get him a room where he could lie down, and I sat with him, just talked to him, stroked his hands for about an hour before he could do the Radio One recording. And he did it. I don't know how. Everyone said, when he came out of the room with me, 'God, what have you done to him?' because he was a completely different person. And then he did it all in one take, it was amazing.

Shaun was the worst the night before Hereford. He was really shitting himself, saying, 'I can't do it,' and all that crap. I don't know what I said to him but I know he said 'Thank you' afterwards.

SHAUN: On the first night of the first gig, me bottle was going. A shipment of valium had to be brought up and I still had enough energy to run a mile.

I wasn't worried about our performance, because we were well intact. You know, I got sick of singing those same old songs years before, but seven years later or whatever it was those old songs started sounding great again, so it wasn't a lack of confidence in the band or the songs, just basic nerves, which I still always get to this day. I get terrible stage fright, really bad. Firstly, now I've got older I don't like dancing and moving on stage and shit like that, I just feel I'm too old for wiggling my hips and dancing and all this sort of shit, it's just one of them things, you know. If you've sold 50,000 tickets and everyone is coming there to see you, that should boost your confidence. But you still get freaked out by it.

Secondly, I've never, ever really enjoyed the thought of playing live gigs. I like them when they've finished and its gone, that's great, but I don't enjoy performing them. I'll put everything into it, and the best gigs are the ones when I'm not conscious of anything that's going on, not thinking about it at all and just in a zone where I'm totally into it. If you're on stage and you're thinking through it, thinking step-by-step, thinking, We're doing this song next and that song after that, we've got an hour and a half, now an hour and twenty, how long have we been on – if you're clock-watching or worrying about your performance then you're not going to enjoy it.

The ones you do enjoy are the ones where you don't think anything, and before you know it, it's over and done with. Drugs can do that, but drugs for me were there way before the music business. In fact the music business was just another way of getting drugs and taking drugs, you know what I mean. I do get to that point where I'm getting nervous before I go on stage and just taking the drugs to block that out.

The journey to Hereford took about three hours of wet grey motorway. But the excitement was building now. Spliffs were rolled, cans were cracked. Various other substances were sorted. Then, as the band arrived at the Grand Hereford Bowl, Neil handed out the laminate passes which go around your neck and give you access all areas.

The newly re-formed Happy Mondays walked in to find their dressing room. Eventually they discovered it, nestled in between a broom cupboard and a makeshift canteen. To say it was small would be an understatement akin to saying Sporty Spice is just a bit of a boot. It was about 10ft by 8ft with a table, a coolbox, four chairs and a TV brought in by special request because of the Manchester United match against Juventus in the Champions League that night.

Obviously this was no good and the Mondays weren't having it. Sod the gig, there was no way they could all watch the footie in this tiny space. The band's master technicians were called in for a sharpish re-wiring job and the TV was moved into the dining area while the band soundchecked. The telly was set up and people were slowly starting to gather around the fold-away wooden tables with wipe-clean tablecloths and hand-written menus put out by the catering crew.

Earlier in the day Shaun had decided he needed a haircut, so a girl from SJM rang around all the hairdressers in Hereford (there's only about six) and found one willing to come and do it. When she turned up and tried to find a room backstage to crop his mop, she chanced upon three rooms next to each other, hidden among the maze of backstage passages and miles bigger and nicer than the tiny dressing room. On the doors, though, were signs which read 'BEZ'S GUESTS'. 'Would you look at that cheeky bastard,' said Shaun.

It wasn't long before support band Shed Seven turned up and Neil got to work pinning the running orders on to the walls.

They read:

7.00:	Doors and kick off
7.45:	Shed Seven (expect a short set tonight because Rick Witter is a mad Reds fan)
9.45:	Happy Mondays onstage

It was all systems go apart from the fact that Paul Ryder was missing, having opted to drive rather than come on the bus with Shaun and the others. But all things considered, it was a miracle things had come this far.

It was 6 p.m. and a bailiff had arrived with a photographer from the local paper to try and serve a writ on Shaun from Nicholl and Dime management. This was an ongoing dispute, which is still unsettled, and so for legal reasons I'll avoid writing what Shaun said about the pair. Enough to know it rhymed with hunts, prats, hits, anchors, birds and lots of others I can't think of rhymes for. Neil managed to talk the bailiff into leaving the writ on the step of the bus. He knew this would mean it hadn't been properly served, and as predicted it was laughed out of court. So Nicholl and Dime's hapless bailiff was forced to follow the Mondays around on their reunion tour, trying unsuccessfully to serve the writ. He was next to make his appearance at Brixton, with hilarious results.

At 7.00 everyone was in the kitchen for the Manchester United kick-off. There were a lot of people milling about now; the hairdresser and her boyfriend had been given access all areas passes and were both propped up against a wall enjoying the free beer. Some of Bez's mates had arrived, and for everyone there the football was more important and demanded more attention than the fact that the Happy Mondays were about to play their first live gig for six years. Cheers went up when a certain person arrived carrying a video cassette. After acquiring a screwdriver from a technician he proceeded to undo the cover of the film and produce a huge block of Colombian marching powder from within, much to the joy of all present. Especially Alan Leach, the Shed Seven drummer, whose meeting with Shaun came as something of a surprise . . .

ALAN LEACH: My first experience of Shaun was before our first night, at Hereford. He opened the dressing-room door as I was walking past, and beckoned me in. So I went in and I was a nervous wreck because I was totally in awe of Shaun Ryder. I spilled my beer everywhere. He emptied a massive bag of coke on to the table and started chopping it out. Then he looked at me and he goes: 'Pop star or peasant?' and I didn't have a clue what he was on about so I said 'Drummer', and he goes: 'One drummer coming up.'

So he chopped it out and it looked good. I'd been off drugs for a while and making a point not to, but that was the beginning of the four days that ruined me for about a month. He chopped it out and there were lines for everyone else in there, and loads left over. I couldn't believe it. It was a massive bag! So when everyone had a line he said: 'Right, does anyone else need sorting or shall I put this away?' Someone said 'Nah, sorted Shaun, put it away' – and he just got a note and snorted the lot! It was more than I've ever seen one person do in my life. So someone said to Shaun, 'I thought you were going to put it away!' and he just went, 'Nah man! I meant put it AWAY!'

Now the Sheds were ready to go on, and the crowd were getting restless. Despite the distraction of the footie, on they went, to get the crowd in the right mood for the Mondays' first performance of their reunion tour. They got the crowd tapping their toes and helped pass the time. The punters gave them cursory claps as they trotted out hit after hit before

Rick Witter made a mad dash backstage, thereby scotching any chance of an encore, in order to catch the last few minutes of the match.

Manchester United, as reported, had made a miraculous comeback. Now everyone was buzzing and it was time for another one.

NEIL MATHER: Hereford wouldn't have worked if United hadn't come from 2–0 behind. You have to think the gods were smiling on us; that gig could have been a disaster if the whole band wasn't buzzed up by that brilliant comeback. For the first ten minutes of watching that match everyone was suicidal, but I think it gave everyone a real focus.

The whole thing was already running 30 minutes later than it should have been because everyone was shitting it about the match going into extra time. But as soon as it was over and Manchester United were going full steam ahead to Barcelona, that was it.

That's why the next gig, the Manchester gig, I'd thought, Fucking hell we need something to play out to, and of course we settled on 'Barcelona', by Freddie Mercury. Everyone picked up on it, from the fanzines to the *NME*.

But for now, this was it, no more bullshit. No more waiting around. It was time to face the crowd. The intro music put together by Ben featured the trademark *'Higher!'* vocal scream from the beginning of 'Hallelujah', latched together with an undulating synth sub-bass sound which sent tremors through the crowd and made the hairs on the back of your neck stand on end.

Shaun was first on the stage in his Adidas cap and sunglasses, the trademark uniform of the tour.

The whole crowd's arms were already in the air, and the tiny hall was showing its appreciation. Shaun had one ear taped up with an earphone inside to help hear his voice better, Rowetta was waving her pom-poms in the air, and Bez began his baggy St Vitus' dance as they launched into the first number – a tempo-shifted fuller-sounding 'Loose Fit'. It was the Mondays as they had only ever sounded on record before. The bass and the drums kicked in together and Wags suddenly became part of the music, his nine-note guitar riff intro condensing the air and dripping nostalgia on to the heads of the crowd.

Then, over the top of the new percussive sound Ryder chipped in, bang on cue, with his opening gambit. His melodic meanderings composed years before completed the sound, and the whole crowd was moving. As if suddenly remembering why they were here, they jumped in a composite freestyle anarchy of stretching limbs and bobbing heads. By the time 'Holiday' was being played mobile phones in the crowd were being held in the air as people called friends or family, crystallising the moment, converting it to binary digits and then sending it through the ether to prick the memory of whoever.

The show was a storm, finishing with 'Step On', with no let up from the crowd until the band returned for an encore. 'Hallelujah' and 'Wrote For Luck' sent them into a frenzy, before a semi-bungled version of 'The Boys Are Back' for the encore. It was a poor finish to a great show in which the atmosphere had been built up into a Bacchanalian fervour, only to be slapped in the chops by the big wet kipper of a poorly rehearsed final number.

The single had been well received overall, getting plenty of play time on the radio, but live it was a complete shambles. And not just on the tour: there were two notoriously shambolic performances on *Top Of The Pops* and *TFI Friday*. The song started off as the final encore, but eventually the decision was made to drop it completely from the set.

> **BEN LEACH:** 'The Boys Are Back' started off as the encore, moved to the middle of the main set, moved about some more before being dropped altogether on the European dates. It was a joint decision from the whole band. My main gripe with it was nobody could play it. I think during the whole time we were playing it we only actually got it right once, and that was in a rehearsal. That may have been due to not having enough rehearsal time with it. It took a lot of time to figure out what was going on in the song, whereas with all the other tracks we'd had loads of time to rehearse them, so they were much tighter.

The crowd, though, seemed not to care and carried on dancing, clapping and shouting for more until the lights came on.

> **GAZ WHELAN:** That gig seemed more like a rehearsal. I think we should have done a few more warm-ups before Manchester, rather than just one night at Hereford; the set went fine, but it was weird, we got the first fucking gig in six years over

with at Hereford in front of a small crowd and then it was like, 'Now we've got to do Manchester.' Fucking hell, just a bit of a difference!

If the Man U game against Juventus hadn't been on I would have been really nervous. But because that game was on and it finished five minutes before we were to go on stage I didn't have time to worry. As it was I was more nervous about the football because United were 2–0 down.

I think it's true to say that game was the saviour of the whole tour. We had come back to win 3–2, and after the whistle went it was straight into the dressing room, grab a beer and then on to the stage. Everyone was on a real buzz from the game and didn't have any time to think about what they were doing. After Hereford, everyone was just swept along for the rest of the tour, but getting off on that good foot with United winning was probably what saved the whole tour from being a shambles.

Everyone was nervous. Shaun and Paul had fallen out again in Birmingham because of their nerves, but the game put everyone in such a good frame of mind we just went out and did it. And if Hereford had gone badly we would have been nervous wrecks at Manchester.

KEITH ALLEN: I used to see Shaun up in the Hacienda when I was up there filming *Making Out* and that's kind of how I got to meet them all. I used to hang about with Bez more than with Shaun really and Bez phoned me months before and told me when the gig was.

I was in Cardiff doing *Jack Of Hearts* and I drove up there in my cab, fuck knows how far it is. Took me about an hour though. It was the night United played; there was a fantastic atmosphere backstage. I hit a pub in Hereford beforehand, and when I walked in United were two-nil down. Then I managed to get into the gig and got backstage just as the third goal went in – it was fucking brilliant. Everyone was going insane.

The gig was fantastic. The Mondays could actually play. They had become a better band and it was a bit of a shock really. I remember being on the phone to my mate and saying, 'Listen to this!' and holding my phone up so he could hear.

There was no real after-show party to speak of, just a lot of slaps on the back and sniffs up the nose in and around the dressing rooms. Oh, and there was a real slap on the arse too, dished out from soul diva Row to one of the cheeky Shed Seven lads:

ALAN LEACH: On the first day of the tour at Hereford we were all a bit in awe of the Happy Mondays, so we were talking to them one at a time trying to get to know them and Rowetta was getting quite chatty and we were getting to know her, and maybe being a little bit cheeky because she was a lady, so she was a bit easier to be cheeky to than the rest of them. Then she got her whip out and Tom dared her to whip him on his bum. She said, 'Pull your pants down then!' He thought she was just like going to have a laugh, so he pulled his pants down and bent over, and I have never heard such a loud scream. He stopped being quite so cheeky after that. At that point Shaun, who hadn't said much until then, jumped out of the dressing room and shouted, 'Ay! Some people pay a monkey for that!' whatever a monkey is.

At about 2 a.m. it was back on the bus up to Manchester for Friday night's show at the Manchester Evening News Arena. On the bus everyone slept, and once it arrived at the Arena at about 5 a.m. taxis were called for everyone except Shaun, who stayed on the bus.

My employers the *Daily Sport* wanted me in for work the next day, so after about three hours' sleep I made my way in, sorted Shaun's column out for the Friday paper and buggered off again to catch some kip.

Manchester was the big one. The homecoming. A gig at the 18,000-seater MEN Arena which hadn't even been built last time the band were playing together. Way back in 1993 it was just a shamble of broken buildings next to Manchester's oldest railway station, Victoria. Now it was home to gigs by the Spice Girls, The Manics, you name it – even Meat Loaf.

Shaun had spent the past two days on the bus as riggers put together the stage and lighting for the biggest indoor gig of the tour. Looking out from the stage into the vast and empty arena, all the different aspects of the gig were coming together. Attendants and security men in yellow jackets stood around being briefed by a fat fellow with a moustache. Then they headed off for their various points at entrances and exits on each of the three levels. About 250 feet above our heads some nutter was playing at Spiderman crawling around among the roof girders and wiring up speaker stacks suspended on cables, before abseiling down to earth again. Then there were lighting people rigging up the stage and the giant Happy Mondays backdrop. Backstage, however, things were a lot messier.

Requests for guest list tickets were getting ridiculous. Neil had set a limit of 90 each for the whole band and had given them each a bundle of tickets for friends and family. Which is where some of them went. Others went to the touts as has long been the tradition of the Mondays who, in typical style, had cottoned on early in their careers that it was more profitable to tout their own guest list, and also to make and sell their own T-shirts outside the gigs too.

Anyway now Neil was getting hassled by Bez and some of the sponsors, as well as everybody else on earth who knew his mobile phone number. Helping him to keep order was the number two security guy for this gig and the London dates, none less than Clifton Mitchell, one of Britain's leading heavyweights in the early nineties and a favourite contender for the national title before being knocked out by James Oyebola in 1994. Despite his credentials as being well 'ard, he was in fact as mild mannered as Penry the mild-mannered janitor from *Hong Kong Phooey*.

But in Manchester, despite the concerns of the local police, things didn't turn nasty.

NEIL MATHER: Manchester was probably the best gig, but it was a lot of trouble more than anything. The arena people were panicking because they were expecting a big fucking kick-off, that's why there was a load of police searches and all sorts of shit going down, but in the end it was like a carnival out there. The only trouble was right at the end when people were trying to get backstage, but that's to be expected.

It was the biggest gig of the tour and there were over 15,000 people plus guests. We said to everybody, 'Right, you can have 90 guests,' but all that went out of the window. On the actual day I was giving Bez 100 tickets at a time and telling him to get out there and do whatever he had to do.

It's not a problem with guest lists at places like the arena; there's always a seat to be had. When you've got the stage at one end, you can sell 15,000 good seats and then you get some seats which are a little bit iffy which are OK to put guests in.

I'd said when we arrived that the best thing that could happen was for Shaun to fall asleep on the bus for two days which is just what did happen. He didn't move and basically had his own private bus.

What I had never experienced was Shaun's nerves before, and what I didn't know was that once he'd conquered that then he'd be fine, and after Manchester he *was* fine. He'd got it behind him and realised he could do it, and I didn't have to worry about him after that.

Doors opened at 7.30 p.m. with the Mondays on at about 10 p.m., and outside the crowds were psyching themselves up for the experience. Fans coming to gigs at the MEN Arena usually arrive via Victoria station next door, where there are bus stops, tram stops and trains, and tonight the concourse was heaving with flares, T-shirts with the *Bummed* cover, or which read 'Hallelujah' or 'Madchester'. Some were newish and worn by fresh-faced teens hiding spliffs in the sleeves of their coats. Others were faded, bought the first time around, pocked with blimp holes and worn by twenty- to thirty-somethings with reddening faces and beer bellies. Everywhere an eager air of anticipation hung over the crowd like the big cloud of skunk smoke which gave them all the same knowing grin.

The crowd was a crowd like few others. It could have been the Rolling Stones playing, to look at the cross-section of ages that stretched across the generations from early teens to forties.

The touts were touting, 'Any spare tickets?' The fans were joking, 'You're twisting my melons, man' and a few beggars were scrounging as everyone made their way through the concourse or from Trinity Way on the other side of the building, and into the arena where former Hacienda DJ Bobby Langley had taken over from Paul Oakenfold for the night to warm up.

Backstage things were going more smoothly. Shed Seven had gone on to play their support slot at 8.15 p.m. and everyone was getting a bit twisted on the rider in the dressing room. Which was infinitely better than the Hereford dressing room, having not only an en-suite bathroom, but loads of beer and one of those mirrors with lights all round the outside that you see in the movies.

Bez arrived with his wife Debbie and their two children. He slipped into his Dr Martens shorts, Admiral T-shirt and Adidas sunglasses and began to limber up. This was a ritual undertaken by Bez before every show. It consisted of a string of warm-up exercises which were in part borrowed from lessons at his local gym, and in part completely made-up Bezisms. They started gently enough, with stretching of the legs, limbering backwards and forwards to warm up the calf and thigh muscles and hopefully avoid any injury while leaping round like a loon on stage. Next came some fairly energetic arm-windmilling. Finally Bez would work on the neck; rolling his head round his shoulders and his eyes around in his head, mouth open, usually while trying to have a conversation with someone. But finally he'd do all three things at the same time and, without any disrespect to Bez, he did look a tit, with his legs stretching, arms flailing, gob open and neck rolling. Actually he looked dangerous. Especially as most of the time this exercise took place in the dressing room, a very confined space. It sometimes looked like he was in the middle of performing a special move from *Streetfighter II*; the sort of move where you have to hit all the buttons on the control pad in a special sequence and requiring fourteen fingers, each with seven knuckles and a jet-pilot's sense of timing.

The rest of the band were milling around the dressing room when the call came to go on stage. Passages were cleared, doors held open, the house lights went low and the crowd went wild as Shaun, Bez, Row, Paul, Wags, Ben, Gaz and Nuts (ever the maverick, in his Manchester City shirt) marched behind the curtain and on to the stage to be met by the deafening cheers of the crowd. It had been a long time coming but it was looking good.

The 18,000-capacity Manchester Evening News Arena (formerly known as the Nynex) had been turned into a 16,000-seat/standing room venue for the night. There were some seats occupied by the older, twenty- and thirty-something old fans; the originals, who had got a bit older and decided they could do without the bother, heat and bustle of the crowd. Gangs of lads and couples: the Hacienda ex-pats. The standing space in front of the stage was crammed with teens, eager-eyed, foaming at the mouth and probably pilled-up to the tits.

A huge psychedelic curtain with the words 'Happy Mondays' covered the front of the stage. And as the arena lights dimmed the crowd's cursory applause fermented into an eardrum-bursting, full-on frenzy of noise, as intoxicating as pure MDMA. Behind the back-lit curtain you could make out the shape of Shaun and co. as they took up their positions at their mikes and instruments. The tumultuous salutations of the crowd rose again as the dizzy acid danceline of the synth lifted their arms and eyes skyward. Then as Paul Ryder and Gaz Whelan began to lead into the cheeky funk-pop of 'Loose Fit', 15,000 people started to move. And as Wags kicked in for the second time that week with the sweet but simple electric guitar, a nine-note flanged elegy, not one person was sitting. The boys were back in town and Manchester was loving every second of it.

The difference between Hereford and Manchester was not only the size of the crowd, but that in

Manchester nearly everyone seemed to know the words, and many were punching the air with each one as projectors sent multicoloured 'Happy Mondays' signs spinning around the arena.

It was like seeing your favourite football team on their best form. Each song was just goal after goal, through 'God's Cop', 'Kinky Afro', 'Rave On', 'Stinkin' Thinkin' – even 'Boys Are Back', which had been moved forwards in the set to keep the crowd riding high and didn't sound too bad. Here and there Shaun spoke, thanking the fans, the sponsors, everyone.

'Hallelujah' and 'WFL' closed the show after fourteen songs. The band were joined on stage by Bez's kids waving a little pair of maracas. It was a great homecoming for them all.

And a crowd, spanned by generations, who would avoid each other in a pub, club, at a party or in the street were brought together for 90 magical minutes. And after those 90 minutes, as Freddie Mercury's 'Barcelona' rang out across the arena in tribute to Manchester United's Champions League final, they left again, peacefully, happy to have been a part of history.

PD: I wanted to go to the Nynex gig because I've never been to the Nynex to watch a band, so the Mondays would have been the apt choice I suppose. But I didn't in the end, and I'm glad now. Well, I'm not glad, I think there was something on I was doing that night.

After the gig there were two parties backstage: one for close family and friends and one for other guests for whom there was no room in the dressing rooms. And while everyone wanted to tell the band what a good job they'd done out there, the Mondays were more interested in getting to say hello to the former Manchester United goalie Peter Schmeichel and team-mate Paul Scholes who had been watching the show and came backstage. Lee Mullen had in fact been giving drum lessons to Schmeichel and introduced everyone to the goalie. It was an eager queue of Mondays who lined up to shake the hands which just two days before had been keeping the Italians' best efforts out of the net.

Friends and family of the band crammed out of the dressing room, but the celebrations were perfunctory and short-lived as the band had to head off up to Scotland. Shortly after 2 a.m. it was on to the buses and up to Glasgow. Once again everyone was pretty much spent by this time and slept most of the way to the SECC. Most people, that is, apart from Paul Ryder and his girlfriend Angela, whose naked backsides made regular appearances between the curtains of their top bunk.

An extra night had been put on at Glasgow because ticket sales had gone so well, and after spending the morning at the venue it was off to the Copthorne Hotel for four hours' kip before sound-check.

It was at the Copthorne that Martin Herbert, the Mondays' otherwise quiet and unassuming guitar technician, hit the front pages. He opened his door stark-bollock naked while on the phone to Neil. Unfortunately, on the other side of the door was a timid Brazilian chambermaid called Maria. Upon being confronted with Martin in his full glory, she dropped her bucket and ran screaming down the corridor, not stopping until she found the hotel manager, whereupon she haltingly told him of the big man with his 'Richard' hanging out, chattering and laughing into his left hand. It emerged that she wasn't too familiar with the concept of cellular phones.

Despite his apologies, Martin was ordered out of the hotel by Neil and made to sleep on the crew bus. Amazingly, Martin agreed to pose for a photo after the tale had done the rounds and the next day he found himself on the front page of the *Daily Sport* under the rather flattering headline of 'Martin's 10-Incher Gets The Chop'. To this day Martin is still known as King Dong, and whether it's true or not, only Maria and Mrs Herbert will ever know.

The backstage area at Glasgow's SECC was separated from the main auditorium by just a curtain and a door, and the band had to make a dash across the main passageway from the outside to get on stage. The dressing rooms were situated next to each other along one corridor, which went to the stage at one end and to the coach at the other.

Bez, who was necking pure MDMA for the shows, preferred the lights and stereo system of the Sheds' dressing room to the mellow chilling chatter of the Mondays' area, and would spend the night flitting between the two, having performed his warm-up, of course.

ALAN LEACH: Bez kept coming into our dressing room, I don't know why but he seemed to like it. He was telling Tom about how he had been doing his circuit training, and there he was, stood in the passage touching his toes and looking proper healthy. Tom came in and said, 'Bez is really healthy, he's been doing circuit training and things and that.' Suddenly we heard a noise, so we stuck our heads out of the door and there Bez was in the corner puking into a bin, puke what looked like tar, and Tom said he'd never seen owt like it. It didn't look like sick at all it just looked like black tar.

That came from Thomas, so if Bez is going to give us a beating for it I want him to know where it came from.

Glasgow carried on the vibe. The only real difference was that this was the only place where the 'Happy Mondays' curtain actually worked. It hung in front of the stage, and the band came on stage behind it, unseen by the crowd. Then, as soon as they began to play over the intro and the bass kicked in, it was supposed to drop down. Whoosh. Straight down to the floor where roadies were waiting to gather it up and take it away. This hadn't worked in Manchester, or in Hereford, where the curtain had had to be raised instead for fear of covering the entire band in canvas when it was released from the ceiling.

Things went pretty smoothly for the next couple of days. The gigs were sell-outs, the reviews were great. On the Friday night the band shared the bar with a wedding reception and Paul Ryder celebrated his 35th birthday by getting everyone to buy him champagne. Ex-Smiths bassist Andy Rourke turned up to say hello and Shed Seven finally said goodbye.

Then it was off to London on the bus. A mind-numbing six-hour journey aboard a bus which was starting to smell a bit like boiled cabbage. Despite the best efforts of the driver, who remade the beds every day, and tour manager Neil, who made sure everyone had clean laundry and would probably have even darned your socks if you asked, there comes a point when a bus with twelve blokes on board becomes a bit whiffy, no matter how clean they are. It's a combination of things, not least bad diet and beer. The smell in the bus would eventually get much worse, but that was later.

Eventually the bus arrived at the posh hotel in Knightsbridge. It was Monday, and there was no gig until Tuesday at Brixton Academy. Bez had arranged for a few of us to go and visit his mate's restaurant later that night, but it was afternoon now and time for some kip.

For days the *Daily Sport* newsdesk had been screaming for some 'Tits out' pictures on the tour. 'Get someone from the audience and get them to get their tits out,' said news editor Paul Carter every time my phone rang. 'Get Ryder shagging some groupies, we need some tits now.'

Now I don't know if these sound like reasonable requests to you, but they are just the tip of the iceberg for Carter. He has what we at the *Sport* called a 'Fred Talbot's Weathermap' view of the world. Fred Talbot is the weatherman on *This Morning* – the one who jumps about on the floating map of Britain, moored in Liverpool's Albert Dock. Well, Carter's brain resembles this map, and Fred Talbot is his thought process leaping seemingly hundreds of miles from the real and probable world to one where fairies and goblins live in a single instant, without any regard for the actual real-life obstacles which lie in your way. It is probably his inability to see these obstacles which have made Carter a good editor. But it's no fun when you're on the other end of the phone to his feckless demands. And the thought of the young women who had come to see one of their favourite bands in concert getting their breasts out was like leaping gracefully from Newcastle to Cardiff. It wasn't going to happen.

Being a dedicated journalist, though, I tried. Once or twice. Well, exactly once, actually. There they were, three girls all bubbly and full of fun, having a great time. They'll be up for a laugh, I thought, so I asked if they'd be kind enough to help me keep my job, and explained what I needed them to do. They looked at me like I was a piece of shit. And I felt they had every right to. But I had to ask, I was being paid.

So anyway I had tried once, I felt justified in letting the *Sport* pay me for that, but I began thinking there must be some better way to give the paper what they wanted . . . and there was.

Inspiration struck once more in the form of Shaun Ryder. We were chatting that afternoon in the hotel about the paper wanting some sort of orgy to happen. I wasn't sure how he'd react and didn't want to suggest anything which would piss him off, or upset my rather strange position as official writer-in-residence, but suddenly he blurted out, 'Well, let's fucking make one, then.'

I didn't need telling twice. Immediately I got on to a couple of girls who'd worked for the paper in the past and had no qualms about exposing their breasts for the cameras. I explained that we were after a simulated orgy scene. They were well up for it.

Within three hours both girls had arrived; one, Jo, travelling down from Yorkshire and another, Hanna, from North London. We all met in the bar, where thanks to a rather generous expense account I was able to purchase 'props' for the 'orgy' in the shape of a case of Budweiser and a couple of bottles of white wine.

Shaun was ready and willing and had recruited Nuts to join in on the action. Bez had politely declined on the grounds that Debs would kill him.

And so it was we retired from the bar of the Knightsbridge hotel, up to an empty bedroom where the Page Three girls stripped for action and climbed on to the bed. Shaun and Nuts rather cautiously climbed in amongst the heaving bosoms and naked limbs and somehow managed a smile for the camera as I snapped away with a Sureshot.

Beer cans and wine bottles were strewn around the room and the bed to give the impression of a drunken party which was descending into debauchery as the girls sat astride the blokes, tweaked their nipples to make them erect, and pouted for the camera.

All in all the shoot lasted about five minutes; then it was down to the bar for a beer. But when I told the *Sport* the next day, they were gobsmacked.

'You wouldn't believe what happened last night,' I told Paul Carter on the newsdesk.

'What, what?' said Carter, his mind zipping from Land's End to Grimsby, via Essex where light showers would be followed by sunshine.

'Ryder and Nuts only trapped off with two Page Three girls they met down at a bar, brought them back to the hotel and had a four-in-a-bed romp,' I said in my best tabloid speak.

'Have you got pictures?'

'I got pictures of the girls topless on the bed with Shaun and Nuts before I got booted out of the room.'

'Fucking brilliant! I'm sending a bike to pick them up – can you file about 25 paragraphs of copy over a.s.a.p.?'

And so it was the next day the *Daily Sport* ran the front page: 'Happy Mondays Sex Romp With Busty Lesbo Babes', much to the amusement of everyone else on the tour.

In fact, the paper was becoming required reading by the entire crew and was being ordered in as a morning paper at the hotel reception. Which is probably a first at one of Knightsbridge's poshest hotels.

After the 'orgy' the girls went home and Bez took the rest of us out to his mate's restaurant, where free food and champagne were laid on, which was impressive enough. But the freaky man had to go one better just to completely impress the arse off us. And after having a quiet word in the ear of a waiter he sat there with a fat ear-to-ear grin on his mullet while everyone else wondered what the fuck he was up to. But before you could say, 'Bez, you cheesy grinning monster', the waiter re-appeared with a covered silver platter which he delivered to Bez, lifted the lid and . . . lo and behold, underneath was a wrap of dark paper containing around a gram of Colombian marching powder! Now, *that's* rock'n'roll.

From the restaurant, we all caught a cab to London's most famous celebrity haunt, the Met Bar. The glitz palace of the capital, where admission is strictly by membership or celebrity status, and where a permanent pack of paparazzi stand outside and bestow their flashbulb blessings on the current media darlings and let yesterday's faces pass by anonymously. I thought I'd give it a go and try to pull a Spice Girl. But they weren't in that night. Your loss, girls.

Monday and Tuesday were mainly spent visiting sponsors around the capital to stock up on free clothes and trainers. Nuts went the maddest, managing to squeeze in Admiral, Dr Martens and Adidas in one afternoon and having to take a black cab back to the hotel because he couldn't carry all his goodies. That's one of the great things about being in a band. People just throw their clothes at you in the hope you'll wear them during your next photoshoot. I don't mean that in a Tom Jones/women's knickers throw-them-at-you kind of way, more the promotional companies who send whole wardrobes-worth of gear to hotels. Bez delighted in telling me he has a wardrobe full of socks and one wall of his house is lined with boxes of Adidas and Nike trainers. Lucky me, I managed to come away with the glorious haul of two Admiral T-shirts and three pairs of Kangol boxer shorts.

Late on Tuesday afternoon, it was time to visit the Brixton venue and complete the soundcheck. Transport to the gig was in a mini-bus which would return to the hotel in the evening to collect Shaun, Rowetta and Nuts. During the ride over, the following conversation took place between Bez's mates Scully, Dermot and Winker, and Gaz Whelan. It was picked up on by Shaun later that day, who included it in his column for the *Daily Sport*. Disturbingly, it brought in more letters than any other subject he's tackled before or since. It went something like this:

Scully: 'You know what really puzzles me? Why the fuck don't you see white dog shit any more?'

Others: 'You what?'

Scully: 'White dog shit! Remember ten years ago you'd always see it, on the street, in the park, fucking wherever. Well, where's it gone?'

Gaz: 'Yeah I remember it, fuck me I haven't seen any for ages either, it used to be everywhere, didn't it.'

Scully: 'Exactly.'

Winker: 'Scully, have you got fuck all better to do than go around observing what style of dog shit happens to be in at the moment?'

Scully: 'Fuck off.'

Dermot: 'It's all down to diet because nobody feeds their dogs bones any more, and that's where all the white used to come from, from the bone.'

Gaz: 'Is that true?'

Dermot: 'I don't fucking know.'

Unfortunately this exchange of views was cut short by our arrival at the venue before any definitive sort of answer could be given. Other hypotheses postulated that afternoon for the pale poo's sad decline from the nation's streets included its use as a fuel for alien space crafts, better street cleaning and various other dietary matters. When Shaun mentioned it in his column one reader was happy to prove that it still existed by sending in a sample he had scooped from a pavement outside his house. Which was nice.

WHITE DOG POO POSER

Here's a question to ponder. Can anyone tell me why you don't see white dog poo on the pavement any

---

more? Everyone has got to remember this stuff, kids who couldn't afford a football used to play 'wallie' with it. But now it's all gone and I want to know where.

Have dogs stopped crapping? Have the council finally got round to cleaning it up? Or maybe somewhere there's a secret society who go around scooping it all up when everyone else is in bed? The poop is out there . . . we should be told.

Finally the stage was set for the London gigs. Paul Ryder insisted on a private bar being put on stage for use during the performances. This consisted of a barrel of Red Stripe lager and a pump so he could pull himself a fresh pint or two at the beginning of each song. Each barrel held around 70 pints and through no mean feat he managed to get through two whole kegs of the stuff by the end of the week, with just a little help from the backline crew.

There were a few famous faces turning up backstage to wish everyone well. Bobby Gillespie from Primal Scream was a regular in the dressing room, and Damien Hirst showed up on the final Thursday night and presented Bez with a shaking stick made out of a real human skull to wave around on stage. A Damien Hirst original! This replaced the voodoo stick Bez had previously been using, a gift from Row. The skull-stick, as it became affectionately known, was the result of a rather intense conversation between Bez and Damien at an earlier meeting. Bez had heard about this big cheese voodoo guy who used to lead people in dancing rituals with something similar, during which they'd all get completely off their heads. Damien thought it would be a touching gesture to make one for Bez, who sort of does the same thing.

A short time later, while on stage, a rather drunken Shaun, failing to spot the importance of the macabre gadget, lobbed it into the crowd where it was seized upon by a young fan. Bez went potty and sent a team of security out into the audience to recover it. Thankfully it was handed over quite gracefully and the lad and his mates who had found it were given invites to the after-show party.

The skull is locked away in Bez's attic now because it terrifies his kids.

BEZ: I met Damien through a pal, Joe Strummer from the Clash, and he's become a really good friend. I told him the idea about the skull maraca I'd been thinking about to make the show more cabaret than it already was.

The idea came from this voodoo geezer who puts people into this ecstatic dance. He was some top voodoo god, you know what I mean. And he holds ultimate power because he holds all the memories of the dead and leads people in this dance. He has rum so powerful that only he can drink it. I was trying to be him, but it didn't quite work.

Loads of people had different ideas about the skull, but then Damien came and gave me this skull maraca which he made for me. It scares everyone to fucking pieces. It looks mad as fuck, man! I had it at Brixton and X slung it out in the audience. I don't know how he got hold of it. I was going to use it out of respect to Damien, and give it a fucking good rattle, but the first thing I'd seen was this skull jumping up and down in the crowd and I thought, 'Eh-up, he looks familiar. So I had to get it back. It was a present.

DAMIEN HIRST: Bez said he wanted a maraca and I had a skull I'd nicked from school. Debs told me he was trying to make one out of a metal skull or something and I just remembered that I had a real one that I nicked and that I'd had lying around for ages. I was pissed up one night so I filled it with mung beans and screwed a broom handle into it, bit of black gaffa tape, drew on a 'stop and go' symbol, and there you are.

The skull was always this thing that was kind of hanging around, it seems to follow you around and I'd never really used it, I just thought that would be a great thing to do with it. But it's a bit too heavy and doesn't sound that great, it's more kind of a thing. But I just thought if Bez is going to have a skull he can have a proper one.

I was at Brixton and I thought the gig was phenomenal. It was such a top atmosphere, looking down at the whole audience and the kind of following they've got, it's phenomenal really. But I kind of felt Bez was working like mad, but I didn't know whether the others really kicked off or whether they were being a bit complacent about it.

For the Brixton gigs the set-list stayed pretty much the same as Manchester and Scotland, apart from a few last-minute changes made on a whim. Variety being the spice of life and all that, but no new tunes were added. The band were confident with the set they had, so just tried moving a few things about, such as having 'Hallelujah' and 'Boys Are Back' in the main set and moving 'Step On' to an encore. The first night, however, was marred by technical hitches during the set. At one point there was a keyboard fault, and at another the 'click' which helps drummers keep time disappeared from Gaz Whelan's headphones. This led to delays in between songs on stage, which Shaun filled by loudly abusing Gaz and Paul and threatening to cut the show short. Just like the good old days.

By the end of the week it had all blurred into one long, glorious piss-up. The days are separated in my mind only by the fish dishes which were on the menu on catering, which was tucked away in a small room backstage: Tuesday poached salmon with lemon and dill, Wednesday smoked haddock with potato curry and Thursday battered cod and chips. By Thursday everyone was knackered and terminally hungover and the only option seemed to be to get wasted – again. Shaun ended up in a right state and Kevin Camp the security boss had to personally escort him from the hotel to the venue, where he staggered drunkenly on stage, only to perform a blinding show.

The London crowds showed their appreciation, but got a bit of a bum deal compared to the other gigs. Manchester and Scotland had taken it out of everyone, and the fans went away with mixed sentiments. You learn this from hanging in the foyer afterwards and hearing how many people say, 'Fucking wicked show!' compared to how many grumbled or complained.

There were always more enjoyed it than didn't. Lots more. But London was the only place where not everyone seemed to buzz their tits off.

It was whilst the Mondays were playing at Brixton that Nicholl and Dime tried again to serve their writ on Shaun, with ridiculous and slapstick-style results. This time the bailiff was spotted in the early hours, lingering outside the stage door at the Academy. The bus was parked just fifteen feet away, but this guy was not going to be happy leaving it stuck in the door. He had to place it in someone's hand. Shaun and the team were going to have to run the gauntlet if they wanted to get away from this lad.

NEIL MATHER: The bailiff incident was on the last night, at about 4.30 in the morning. We were expecting it, and all the time we were getting Shaun ready or the Mondays were on stage or whatever, me and Kevin would both take a radio and we'd be on the look-out, even in the hotel lobby, because we expected another attempt. The first one had got laughed out of court on the Monday, so we knew there was going to be another attempt either Tuesday, Wednesday or Thursday.

It was on that last night. I'd got on the bus and I looked out to see these two guys hanging around. So I radioed to Kevin who was in there with Shaun, and told him to check these fellas waiting outside the stage door at 4.30 in the morning.

Clifton, the ex-boxing champ and Mondays security guy, goes out and has a word. Kevin comes back on the radio and says all these guys want to do is get a picture.

I thought something wasn't right. The minute Shaun appeared they were fucking in there. Clifton and Kevin are coming out with Shaun and this bloke's running up to him saying, 'Shaun Ryder, High Court Writ!' and this writ went flying in the air. Kevin and Clifton grab the bailiff, and Shaun's shouting, 'You fucking idiot, that fucking hit me that.' So the bailiff tries to claim he served the writ because Shaun said it hit him.

There were some tense moments, until we realised how to settle the matter. The Brixton Academy has CCTV, so we all had to sit down and watch the video.

Kevin was standing right behind the bailiff, ready to lamp him in case he tried to have a pop at me and then leg it. We all watched the time-lapse video with the rest of ShowSec, the security company, who were clearing up the venue. It was very tense until we got to the point where it happened. I said, 'There it is, in the air. There it is on the floor, case dismissed.' And everyone went, 'Hooray!' then turned to the bailiff and went, 'Wanker!'

Basically what Nicholl and Dime did is they issued on the whole tour itself, so we couldn't pay anyone. There were writs served on SJM, the merchandising company, the venues – everybody. Everywhere you went there was a writ. We couldn't pay any money in connection with Shaun, we weren't even allowed to give him anything at all. That's why I paid all his bills for him, everything. You can imagine this severely hampered everything we could do. But they never

managed to get the final writ served to make
Shaun go to the High Court, because, allegedly,
they ran out of money first!

The final gig of the official tour was Dublin. It took
fucking ages to get there, and the ferry crossing was
traumatic; not because it was a rough sea, but because
the boat was overrun by women rugby players singing
sea shanties punctuated with bursts of 'Swing Low
Sweet Chariot'. These were scary women who all had
necks like Roger Mellie The Man On The Telly and
voices like Pavarotti. Some even had the beard to
match.

As soon as we arrived I crashed out in my plush
hotel room at the Berkeley Court. Bez, Gaz and a
couple of Bez's mates went out to hit the town, but
everyone else just went to sleep. Bez and co. disappeared until 11 a.m. the next day when they arrived
back at the hotel looking pale and in need of sleep.
They had gone down to Temple Bar, Dublin's cool
quarter, and after everything had shut there, had gone
on to a pub which opened at 9 a.m. and were taken on
a brewery tour where they got to sample all the local
ales. All this before 10 a.m.

As well as going on a massive bender, Gaz Whelan
nearly ended up in pokey after being accused of
sexually assaulting a horse while out in the centre of
Dublin with the others. A bit the worse for wear, for
some bizarre reason the conversation turned towards
the size of horses' todgers. In Temple Bar area, a
common sight are the horse-drawn carriages which act
as both tourist attractions and taxis. It transpired that
while *en route* from one bar to another, Gaz became

more than a little over-excited and made a lunge for one of the horse's knobs while declaring: 'Fuck me, look at the size of that!'

The chaos which ensued saw the carriage owner publicly bawling at Gaz and screaming for the Gardaí, as other horse carriages and their owners began to crowd around to take stock of the situation and, probably, lend a hand if things got nasty. Gaz and the others in their inebriated state took immediate stock of the situation which was beginning to cause a great deal of interest among passers-by, made an informed decision as to the most apposite course of action – and legged it.

Of course the incident had to be written up but Gaz was unwilling to put his name to it and stated as a mitigating factor, 'I just wanted to see if it was as big as mine. Fucking hell, it's not like I was having sex with it.'

In the end, Shaun was brave enough to take the rap and give me the story with him as the culprit. A story which ran under the headline 'End Of The Tour ... And Shaun Ryder Feels A Little Horse'.

Later that day we all piled on to the bus which took us to the North Side where the SFX Club was. This part of town looked bad. There was even white dog shit, and a visit to the pub with Paul Ryder and Ben to try out the Guinness ended when a local put out a cigarette in my pint. So I made a beeline back to the venue where security told us to stay inside as crowds had begun to gather outside. There was no catering area here because there wasn't enough room.

The dressing room had boarded-up windows and held three leather sofas with holes where the padding was spilling out. Old posters on the dressing room walls showed people unfortunate enough to have played here in the past; these included Stiff Little Fingers, New Model Army and The Damned, although the SFX probably seemed in a lot better nick in the days when gobbing and wrecking the joint were still cool. A long table lined the back wall and through a broken door at the far end of the room was a toilet which made the best case for outside lavatories I've ever encountered.

The place may have been a bunghole but the crowd were fantastic. And musically the show was brilliant. It's just a shame Bez couldn't appreciate it all because after his all-night bender he was having trouble keeping up his usual freaky style. In fact he seemed to spend most of the show crouched behind one of the front monitors, or round the side of the stage throwing up into a bucket – again.

After the gig it was back to the hotel, via Temple Bar where a friend of Bez (surprise!) had opened up a special area for the band and crew in his bar. But as soon as the free booze ran out everyone piled back to the hotel to hit the bar there. It sounded a good idea in theory, but the reality of the situation turned out to be a bit different as two decrepit barmen found themselves swamped as around 100 wide-eyed crew, band members and hangers-on descended upon them. These two refused to serve anyone without a keycard for the hotel. This, of course, led to the swapping, lending and borrowing of said items around the party and a few shocked faces the next morning when everyone discovered what they had paid for.

The day after the Ireland gig everyone was rounded up and herded on to the coach for the trip back to

Manchester. I for one had been struck down with terminal heartburn after only a week on the road. God only knows how anyone can manage it for longer.

But as we all settled aboard the bus to head for the ferryport and our high-speed boat home, something bad happened.

The thing about tour buses is, like everything else in life, they have certain rules. On the one hand they're this incredible twisted world on wheels and the stage for countless scenes of debauchery. But on the other they're a refuge. An oasis of calm in the mad frenzy that is touring. Not just on the road, but when you arrive at a venue. You can live safely behind the smoked glass, away from the fans, the crowds, the security and, in our case, the bailiffs; you can hide from the backstage madness of rigging, cooking, tuning, building and a million short fat blokes in black t-shirts running around wild-eyed, hungover, plugging things in. You're well out of the way. You can chill with a beer, relax in bed, watch a movie or play on the Nintendo, and while the people who design these things obviously go out of their way to make them as comfortable and entertaining as possible, tour buses like everything else also have a downside. I'm not just talking about the fact that you can be cooped up for anything up to twenty hours at extremely close quarters with the rest of the band; not even the fact that as well as being a party on wheels such close contact can inevitably bring out the worst in a lot of people; and not just that while trying to kip on the move you are driven mad by your own thoughts – your dreams change gear every time the bus does and you find yourself in a semi-conscious state mentally charting every turn, every sway and every corner the bus makes. No, it's none of these. In fact, a little psychological trauma can be good for the soul. What really gets you is the *smell*.

Imagine it. On a fourteen-bunk bus, that's fourteen arses primed from a diet of free booze and junk food loaded and ready to fart, fourteen pairs of socks, fourteen lots of undies, twenty-eight sweaty armpits and however many pairs of trainers, every day.

The smell is the reason for the only real golden rule of tour buses. The one immutable law in this small anarchic state on wheels: NO SHITTING ON THE BUS. This has to be obeyed at all costs, at all times and by all people, no matter how big a rock star you are. You just don't do it. Elvis himself would have been keel-hauled if he had ever deigned to drop a deep-fried-banana-butty-bomb into the deep dark blue of the chemical loo. We're talking something similar to a capital crime here. As Shaun explains:

SHAUN: One reason you don't shit on a tour bus is the massive bill from the bus driver, because he's got to clean it. At £350 it's the dearest crap you could ever have. So think about that next time you're at Euston and it costs you 20p. Second is that it stinks out the fucking bus. I mean the toilet smells of piss after a few days anyway, so there's this big unwritten rule that you don't shit in the chemical crapper.

If you've really fucking got to go, and you're travelling along and you can't stop, you open up the skylights on the bus, get a plastic bag, shit in that and fling it out of the sun roof. You just hope

a copper's not behind you, ready to pull you over
to ask, 'Is this your shit, sir?'

The bus is your home. But it's also like a
travelling borstal; you get to know everyone
through their smells. Say a band member was
shagging your missus, you could recognise which
one it was from the smell of their sweat, that's
how close you get. It can send people crazy when
you're in a close environment. It's called
'Submarine Syndrome' – farts, shit, piss can send
people doo-lally.

The no-shitting rule is one of those rules like gravity; if it
isn't obeyed things can really go arse about tit, and when
we were leaving Dublin things *really* went arse about tit.

Nuts was my candidate, but only because he found
it and tried to blame me. The subsequent 'whodunnit'
would have given Hercule Poirot his biggest challenge
to date. Not so much *Murder On The Orient Express*,
more sort of *Turder On The Bus Of Excess*.

The rest of the band were sat upstairs on sofas
watching TV, when Neil, who Nuts had told following
his discovery of the log, broke the news in his own
inimitable way:

Neil: 'Who's fucking shit in the toilet?'

[Blank looks]

Shaun: 'No way, man! No way someone's shit on
the bus!'

Neil: 'Come on, own up you bastards. That's a £350
shit!'

Shaun looked at Bez, Bez looked at Wags, Wags
looked at Lee, Lee looked at Gaz, Gaz looked at
Rowetta and Rowetta looked at me.

'I didn't fucking do it!' said everyone.

Neil disappeared downstairs wondering whose wages to dock the cleaning charge out of. The finger-pointing and recriminations began.

'Wags, you dirty bastard,' said Gaz.

'Fuck you, man, no way would I drop a log on the bus,' Wags hit back. 'I bet it was you, you smelly arse, I bet it's all that Guinness you drank. Neil! Is it black?'

'Come on Wags, spill the beans.'

'He has already!'

Everyone laughed.

'Nuts found it,' said Wags.

'Don't even go there!' Nuts replied.

'Well don't even think of looking at me,' said Shaun. 'Fifteen fucking years I've been on tour buses and I haven't taken a crap on one yet. You just don't do it.'

Then silence again as everyone's eyes turned back to the TV screen. 'The Boys Are Back' video had just been completed and was playing. Abstract bursts of Manchester skyline and landmarks flashed on to the screen amidst footage from the gig at the city's arena and everyone sank back into their own private reveries.

A little bit of trust was gone, as everyone tried to finger the phantom crapper in their midst. It was hard to believe that someone had gone and broken the golden rule. I think a lot of suspicion lay on me, being something of a new boy. But it wasn't. And to this day, no one knows who actually did it.

We arrived back in Manchester at about 5 p.m. I felt like I needed a week off, but I knew I had to face work first thing in the morning, so I headed home in a cab. My girlfriend Rachel greeted me with the kind words one offers to a weary traveller as he returns from a journey into the strangest lands, with the strangest people. She said: 'You look like shit!'

The band were all given two months off through May and June to recover from the gigs and set themselves up for going back on the road again. But one holiday/gig combination they managed to pull off before heading over to Japan at the beginning of July was the Manumission opening party.

It was typical: one of Shaun's Ibiza expeditions, like his infamous *Sport* trip, scheduled for three days and eventually lasting over a week.

The band were put up in the plush Manumission Motel, which boasts water beds and jacuzzis in every room. World-famous dope smuggler Howard Marks was staying there at the same time, and of course he and Shaun hit it off instantly. Shaun had previously contributed to Howard's band Dope Smugglaz' version of the Donovan track 'Barabajagal'. The two had met briefly the year before at the *Loaded* awards, but now had a chance to really find out exactly how much they had in common.

It was the second week of June and Ibiza was getting into the rhythm of the summer. Scores of Brits pour over to the island each year to party the summer away. Some go on holiday; some go to work. Everyone who's anyone, though, goes to Manumission.

Manumission is now more than a club. It's a lifestyle, a hedonistic heaven where anything goes. Part of the infamous superclub's not-so-mysterious appeal is, of course, that each night during the party season they stage live sex shows for the thousands of punters crammed into the place. The people who take part have included Manumission promoters Mike and Claire. Shaun knew the pair from their early days in Manchester when they used to go drinking together at The Rembrandt on Canal Street. Mike and Claire started off by running a small club and bar. When gangsters came asking for protection money they upped sticks to Ibiza where they, somehow, created the phenomenon that is Manumission. During their infamous shows there was sometimes more than one girl with Claire, who's a good-looking and incredibly sweet-natured red-head. They would dress up in latex or nurses' outfits and have sex with Mike on stage while everyone watched and every bloke thought: 'Mike, you lucky, lucky bastard.'

This time around, the Mondays' Manumission gig passed in a blur, with topless dancers distracting Shaun from his singing almost as much as the copious amounts of whisky and pot he'd nailed before the show. After the performance most of the rest of the band headed home to England, but Shaun and Rowetta stayed on the island at the request of Mike and Claire, the owners of the superclub and motel.

Later on during their stay Mike and Claire went with Shaun and a few others out on a friend's yacht sailing from San Antonio bay into some sheltered coves around the coast where people did a bit of skinny dipping. The coves were idyllic: the sea was shimmering aquamarine, catching glancing rays of sunshine in the ripples around the boat. Around the shallow bay it mirrored and blended an upturned world in its reflective calm while gentle waves lapped on to the ivory beach. It was serene, like paradise: azure sky, clear waters, white sands and bronzed bodies.

Then, as everyone dozed on the yacht or splashed in the water, this idyll was suddenly pierced by a sharp, blood-curdling scream. Everyone sprang to their feet. Had somebody been attacked by a shark? Was a murderer on the rampage? 'Aaaaaaaaaaaaaagggggggh! Fuck! *Fuck! FUUUCK!!*' came a cry as twelve people scrambled from their supine sun-worshipping positions on the deck to the prow of the boat. And there was Mike Manumission in the water howling like a ban-shee, jumping around like a jack-in-the-box, and holding his tackle like his life depended upon it. 'My fucking knob!' he screamed. '*My fucking knob!!!*'

Just for the record, it was a jellyfish. But Mike still managed to perform for the crowds that night. Now *that's* a man.

After their slightly extended stay in Ibiza the Mondays put in an appearance at Brixton again, but this time for a Comic Relief gig alongside a host of other big names. The dressing-rooms backstage at the Academy were split into three sections: Male, Female and Happy Mondays. Shaun explains:

> **SHAUN:** None of the other cast wanted to go anywhere near our dressing room. For example, that bald feller from *The Fast Show* was after a bottle-opener. I told him there was one in our dressing room and he goes: 'Whoa! Is that safe?'
> But let's start at the beginning. The moment we arrived, Bez fucked off to his mate's bar to watch the football. He spent the whole afternoon getting leathered and so when he failed to turn up we had to send Neil to find him and bring him back.

Now, Bez doesn't normally drink, so when he does he changes completely, and becomes a very happy, smiling drunk.

So we got him back to the gig and he was outside the dressing-room talking to this guy about all sorts of bollocks. Suddenly he realises this bloke is none other than Ali G, so he starts shouting, 'Fucking hell! You're Ali G! Ali G! You're fucking great, you!' Bez then gives the guy a massive bear-hug and proceeds to repeat every line of every sketch Ali G has ever done back to him.

It was a weird crowd there for us because they were all suited and booted and it reminded me of that Sid Vicious 'My Way' video. So I thought it would be a good idea to, er, shoot the audience during the next night's show.

Neil got me a starting pistol. Fuck knows where he got it from, but it was shite. There was me doing my best Tarantino baddy-face. I was going to start by blowing the band away, but the fucking thing jammed, and I was stood there on stage like a cunt, clicking away at them.

Anyway, we finished the set, and Neil had fixed the gun for us when someone said that Ali G was on stage so I thought it would be fun to go and pretend to pop a cap in his ass. I steam out on to the stage to shoot Ali G, but it's not him. It's that fucking bloke who plays Trigger in *Only Fools And Horses*, and you can't shoot him because he's a really nice bloke. Some fucker then tried to drag me off-stage, so I went to shoot them and it fucking well jammed again. Bastard.

June also saw Shaun making a second appearance on Chris Evans' *TFI Friday*. The band had previously been on as a whole for a shambolic performance playing the new single and 'Step On', but this time Bez didn't have any drugs and couldn't get into freaky dance mode. He strutted stiffly around the stage dancing more like a shy mod than a Bez. Meanwhile Shaun played a children's entertainer called Uncle Shaun, who told rude jokes. Lisa Stansfield was on the show too and the pair went out to Epping Forest Country Club to catch up on old times after filming.

> **SHAUN:** I've known Lisa since she was dead little. She knows me mum and me dad and my mum and dad know all their family. We always bump into each other on planes.
> Lisa's family are the only family in the whole of showbiz to make mine sound posh. She always reminds me of when she was little and at the Rainbow Rooms, or *Talk Of The North*, one of them hard-grafting Salford gaffs, and she always came first in the talent shows, whilst my dad, who was trying to be a stand-up comedian at the time, always ended up coming second.

Mohammed Al Fayed was also on the show; Evans introduced him as a look-a-like, and shocked the audience when it turned out to be the real Harrods boss.

> **SHAUN:** It was a shock to find Al Fayed on the show, and you know what? I can't find my passport since that night. Still, he wouldn't get far

with it. Imagine his shock if he tried to get into America with my passport and discovered he'd been done for smuggling porn and been caught with cocaine.

June also saw Shaun, Nuts and Gaz Whelan heading down to Chelsea's Stamford Bridge ground for a celebrity football tournament. Shaun decided against playing and sat on the sidelines working out with a Benson & Hedges before heading up to the bar with Rowetta. I was drafted in to play in goal for Gene and Delakota and managed to let in an incredible thirteen. Having said that, I did save one by Peter Beardsley who was playing with Ant and Dec. Keith Allen's side won the trophy at the end of the day by beating Robbie William's All Stars, which was basically Robbie and a load of ringers he'd drafted in from somewhere. At the after-match party Shaun and Damon Albarn spent the entire evening arguing about who had worn the first Pringle and Burberry clothes.

July saw the band begin the festival circuit around Europe and the Far East. They kicked off with a trip to a festival at Kristiansand in Norway in the first week of July. It was at this point that the whole tour turned into some sort of *Carry On* movie meets *Fear and Loathing*, with the whole band and crew staggering drunkenly from one comic moment to the next. The farce began before they had even got to the airport:

NEIL MATHER: I'd got to bed about 1 a.m. and I had to get up at 7 a.m. to get everyone to the airport to fly to Norway. The phone started ringing at 1.30 a.m., 1.45 a.m., 2 a.m. and I wasn't answering it. 2.15 a.m. and there was a knock on the door. And there was Paul Ryder telling me he'd forgotten his passport. So I had to get somebody from Manchester to drive his passport down in the middle of the night. Anyway I finally got to sleep about 3 a.m., then at 4.15 in the morning the phone rang again: Kevin Camp, the head of security, had got an ear infection. I don't know why he decided he had to tell me at four in the morning, but by the time we got to the airport Kevin had sent his new man along. I got everyone checked in and went off with the security guy to sort out his tickets – and he pulled out his girlfriend's passport instead of his own. Great. And in the meantime Shaun had lost his bag.

By the time we got on the plane to Copenhagen, things were already pretty fucking pear-shaped and I still hadn't had a lot of sleep. We got to the airport without serious mishap, but from there we were supposed to get on a little 50-seater plane to Kristiansand, along with Basement Jaxx and Phats and Small.

Now, Shaun's always the last one on a plane. He won't get on until everyone else is on and he's the last remaining passenger. But as I was finally heading towards the gate with him who did I see but Wags and Gaz heading off in the opposite direction. I said, 'What the fuck are you two doing?' Gaz said, 'Oh, it's been delayed, don't worry about it.' 'No it fucking hasn't, come with us, *now*,' I said, but Wags was already heading off on one of his little shopping trips.

Anyway we got through the gate, and me and Shaun were literally the last two through. Gaz and Wags had fucked off – they were nowhere to be seen, and the ground crew started to shut the gate.

We found the others and got on a little bus to go to the plane. That's when somebody asked, 'Where's Gaz and Wags?' And I just went, 'I don't give a flying fuck any more.' Basement Jaxx said it was the funniest thing they'd ever seen. You could just tell that I'd had a fucking hard time of it by this point. But the next thing there was this tiny little fucking airport truck coming haring after the bus with Wags and Gaz perched precariously on the back.

It turns out Gaz is scared of flying in little planes. So he proceeded to get absolutely shitfaced, and every time we hit a bit of turbulence he'd got his hands in the air going 'Whoaaaa!' like he was on a rollercoaster, and the whole fucking plane was going mad and rocking from side to side all the way into Kristiansand. And that's where Shaun went missing for three days.

We'd done the gig and we were due to leave and I couldn't find him. I'd got all these different sightings of him in different rooms in the hotel at different times of the morning and I was haring round and I couldn't fucking find him at all and it got to a point where I thought, Right, fuck it. I told everyone else to go to the airport, and said I'd just have to stay and find him. Stumpy and Martin (two of the backline crew) were hanging around for a ferry because they were driving back, and so we decided to go and have another look for him

around the town. So who was the first person we
bumped into on the next corner? Shaun, who says,
'Alright there! What's happening?' I said, 'Well
. . . everyone else has fucked off, Shaun, but if we
get a taxi now we can just about make it.' But he
didn't fancy that. 'No, I like it here. Let's stay for
a couple of days' he said. So I just said 'OK.' I
finally found a hotel room, changed the flights and
for the next three days I just kept finding him and
losing him again. There was a big running joke
throughout all the bands who were there who
would see me walking through the streets of this
tiny little town looking for Shaun at all hours of
the day and night.

After a few days it was coming to the point
where it looked like we were going to miss
another flight. But Shaun came staggering in on
the last morning with some dodgy bird on his arm,
saying, 'Fucking hell, it's hard work trying to find
drugs in this town, but I found some.' By this stage
he was ready to drop. He was falling asleep in the
taxi, falling asleep at the check-in; I even got him
first on the plane this time, and as soon as he got
to his seat that was it. It was a proper Scando
babe-fest in Norway though, I must say. The show
was fucking brilliant as well.

In true Mondays style, each gig was characterised by
the antics of certain members of the band rather than
the cultural diversity of the different places they were
playing. In fact most of them will be remembered for
what Wags got up to. For instance rather than
remembering Japan for the saki, the sushi, the fact that

it's the most industrialised nation in the Far East, or the many Buddhist and Shinto temples, it will always be remembered for Wags in a wheelbarrow. In Portugal it's not the traditional dress or the jellyfish which trigger off fond memories, but the Wags' underpants/Peter Schmeichel incident. In fact, Wags pretty much stole the show when he wasn't out shopping. Shopping and Wags go together like Salman Rushdie and death threats. It happens every day and in the end you just get used to it. It doesn't matter what it is, or where it is. He could be in the middle of the Syrian Desert on a religious retreat or living on top of a stone pillar and he'd still manage to go missing for six hours and turn up at 6 p.m. with a load of Moschino shopping bags saying 'Look at this cool watch I got'.

T In The Park passed off peacefully enough, but the Fuji Festival in Japan, for a massive 70,000 people, was a corker. Here Wags was back to his old tricks again; that is, when he wasn't off shopping. The Mondays were headlining the second stage and ZZ Top were supposed to be on the main stage. Neil Mather takes up the story:

NEIL MATHER: We were actually on stage the same time ZZ Top were on, but ZZ Top wouldn't play a note; they said it was too empty because everyone was at the Mondays. Ours was a fucking brilliant set despite the fact that Wags was so pissed he could hardly stand up. It was absolute chaos though, panic everywhere. The Japanese were terrified of us because we had a big fuck-off row with them a few days before, when they pulled out of paying for Bez's girlfriend Debs to fly out despite us having all these emails from them saying they'd do it. Come to think of it, everybody was scared of us. The reputation went before us.

Japan was really a case of Wags in the wheelbarrow. I got Kevin to wheel him to bed after the gig, but the problem was that Kevin took him to the wrong block of the hotel we were staying at. Kevin was lost, and all Wags could say was that he needed a piss, so Kevin left Wags holding the lift while he went for a look around what should have been the right floor. He put Wags' arm against Wags' chest, made a fist with the hand, pulled the index finger out straight and leaned him against the side of the lift so his finger was on the button to keep the lift doors open. Of course when Kevin got back the lift had gone. Kevin had to search every floor until he found Wags about three floors down having a piss behind a vending machine.

The next festival was Portugal on 6 August, for the Sudoeste event, and it was probably the worst gig of the whole lot. We had to travel down dirt tracks for about three hours to get to the venue and there were about forty or fifty thousand there. Despite the numbers, they were the most disinterested crowd I've ever seen in my life. I was going to make it into a bit of a holiday for the band by giving them a couple of days off after the gig, all expenses paid, but Lisbon just turned out to be the biggest shithole on earth. It was dull as dishwater there.

To relieve the boredom, we went to meet Schmeichel again at his debut for Sporting Lisbon.

This was on the last day before we were due to fly back to England, and it produced another fantastic Wags moment.

Wags had gone out and bought a load of absinthe, and drank three quarters of a bottle. On the way back to the airport he was so pissed he managed to lose his plane ticket. Peter Schmeichel was meeting us at the airport because me, Lee and Gaz had been to see him play and he wanted to come and say goodbye. So he's talking to Lee and Gaz, and he says to them, 'Where's Neil, the guy who looks after you?' They pointed to the other side of a big glass wall where I was trying to sort Wags out. Wags, still arseholed, was pulling everything out of his bag and slinging it around the airport, trying to find his ticket. Schmeichel looked at him for a moment, and asked, 'Why is that man throwing all his underpants in the air?'

I had to get Wags a new ticket, and he was so pissed his tiny amount of Portuguese had gone arse-about-tit. Every time he thought he was saying 'Thank you' to the airport staff he was actually saying 'Obrigado,' which is 'Hello!' The woman at the check-in desk was handing him stuff and saying 'Thank you' in English, and Wags was sort of nodding back at her knowledgeably and saying 'Hello' in Portuguese. And I'm trying to shut him up because if they'd realised how pissed he was they wouldn't have let him on the plane.

But amidst all the fun of the tour, Paul Ryder had started dabbling in heroin again, and landed himself with another habit.

PAUL RYDER: I didn't want a habit back. But yeah, I ended up with a fucking habit back. And halfway through the tour I put myself in detox and I've been clean ever since. It was like, yeah I like the music business but I don't want to do it again with a fucking heroin habit so I'll sort myself out and I'll carry on. And that's what I've done.

I couldn't have done it without my mates Disco Dave and Andy. They were a big tower of strength behind me, really encouraging me because it was quite a daunting thing thinking, Oh, we've got to play Nynex and SECC now!, so I'd like to say thank you to them.

What I liked best was coming out of detox and the very next day getting on a plane to Japan and doing my first ever, ever totally clean and totally straight gig with the Mondays, and that was a fucking big buzz.

The next gig was at the Eclipse Festival at Carlyon Bay, in Cornwall. Given all the press about the eclipse – how the roads would be jammed for days, how supplies of food and water were expected to run out, there would be no accommodation to be found anywhere and the army was preparing emergency plans in case of a major catastrophe – Neil very sensibly decided to allow two days' travelling, just in case. A great idea, but seeing as hardly anyone bothered going to Cornwall for the eclipse it was a waste of time.

NEIL MATHER: We expected traffic chaos so we gave ourselves two days to get there and we got there the fucking next morning. There was no cunt there and it was cold.

The whole Cornish festival scene for the eclipse was a farce. So much misinformation had been spread by the local papers and the national press that police were telling party-goers the festivals were cancelled and forcing them to turn around.

This happened at quite a few sites. The attitude of the Cornish authorities stank. It's easy to imagine the council chiefs sat on a bale of hay chewing straw and playing duelling banjos, *Deliverance*-style, and chuckling at the trouble they made for the 'outlanders'. Such was the attitude of the local dignitaries to invasion of tourists into their, er, tourist resorts.

Their trouble-making did for a lot of people, not least Harvey Goldsmith, the promoter who put on Live Aid. He went bankrupt over his aborted eclipse festival at Penzance, because hardly anyone turned up. Most organisers lost money, including the guys at Night Time. A fantastic bunch who worked their arses off for twelve months putting together a show which brought together an amazing line-up of DJs and bands, only to see it all go to pot when no one turned up because they had been scared away fearing some sort of state of emergency.

The V99 festival on August 21 and 22 nearly didn't happen for the Mondays. Earlier on in the month, Shaun was involved in a road accident. He had borrowed a bicycle from Rowetta and was riding along a road in Wythenshawe when a driver allegedly rammed him off the bike and sent him sprawling unconscious on the pavement, leaving him unable to walk properly. Luckily he recovered in time for the gig, though he still had wounds under his tracksuit trousers. And the very day of V99 Shaun was witness to a terrible tragedy in Manchester, and police said they might need him on hand for interviews. At the time he was staying on the fifth floor of the Renaissance Hotel. On the night of the 20th he heard a party going on in the room next door to his. Some salesmen from a conference at the hotel were having a bit of fun; Shaun had no problem with that and went to sleep, only to be woken by a screaming girl hammering on his door in hysterics. The high jinks had turned to tragedy and as the pair of pals fooled around on the window-ledge of the room, they had slipped and tumbled to their deaths 100 feet below. It was Shaun who raised the alarm. The following week he used his column to send messages of condolences to the families of the two men.

The only incident of any note from V99 itself was when Rowetta disappeared for some length of time with a couple of Premiership footballers she met backstage. To this day she's keeping what happened a secret.

The final gig of the year was to be at Slane Castle, near Dublin. It was easily the biggest yet, with a crowd of 80,000 punters crammed into the castle grounds for the day-long show which featured Robbie Williams headlining. The Mondays were third from the top of the bill. Weeks before, Robbie had told a music paper he thought the Mondays should have been the ones headlining the show instead of him. Shaun is one of the few people idolised by the showbiz phenomenon that is Robbie Williams!

Their paths had crossed numerous times. The first time was ten years before, in 1989. They bumped into each other at a Manchester train station where Robbie begged Shaun to sign his tracksuit. Shaun happily obliged and they met again two years later when Robbie was working as a barman in Manchester's trendy Dry Bar, a Factory Records-owned establishment and sister venue of the famous Hacienda club. It transpired that after his shift Robbie was heading off for an audition to join a band called The Cutest Rush with Gary Barlow and Mark Owen, which would later become the world-famous boy-band Take That. 'I wished him all the best with the interview and the next thing I knew he was a superstar,' said Shaun.

Slane was on August Bank Holiday, and as we waited for Bez to arrive at the tour bus outside Neil's hotel in the heart of Manchester's gay village, people were already starting to arrive for the annual Mardi Gras which hits the village like a fleet of fluffy pink steamrollers, only to disappear again leaving hordes of wide-eyed casualties gibbering in doorways from three days of no sleep and an overdose of E, speed, coke and enough amyl nitrate to drown a blue whale.

Things were already starting to get a bit weird and it was only 11 a.m. As we waited by the bus with Neil and security man John Camp, brother of Kevin and co-owner of the security firm, a steady procession of moustachioed men with the bottoms cut out of their leather pants wandered past. A stilt-walker was putting the final touches to a feather head-dress just across the way. Two people were sticking club flyers in the links of a metal fence by the bus and someone else was walking behind them, pulling them out again. And slowly, one by one, the band began to turn up.

Everyone except for Paul Ryder and Wags were coming on the bus to Ireland. Paul because he couldn't face the long drive in such a confined space with his brother, and Wags because he had some shopping to do. Probably. In any case, they had arranged to fly over the next morning in plenty of time for the event.

It was the last gig not only for 1999, but for the foreseeable future. There had been talk of maybe some more dates at Christmas and in the New Year but nothing had been set in stone and, judging by the feeling on the bus, everyone knew this was probably it. And of course the whole band was determined not to let it get them down but to go all out for a good time.

Everyone was in high spirits. There was plenty of whisky, wine and spliffs. *Lock Stock and Two Smoking Barrels* was slapped on the video and a crate of Stella vanished swiftly down various throats.

By the time we got to Holyhead everyone piled into the shop to stock up on more Stella. We had two hours to wait for the ferry and a sort of afternoon-drinking malaise set in. And as it did, evil Eddie and Nuts hatched a plot to liven up the proceedings.

Having spotted me sitting on the bus roof, smoking a cigarette and gazing across the waters they decided that I was fair game for their afternoon's sport. I was perched on the edge of a skylight, with shoeless feet dangling inside the bus. But they were very quickly out of the bus after Nuts took a lighter to an aerosol deodorant and tried to 'flame-throw' my poor feet. I hurled a string of obscenities and, slapping out a small fire in my socks, heard a call from behind. It was Eddie the sound engineer, head sticking through another skylight and urging me to sneak along the top of the bus and back inside through the other hole. Which I did, unbeknownst to Nuts, who was still firing bursts of flame out on to the roof. Of course, you can guess what's coming next. As I crawled precariously and laboriously on all fours between the two skylights, and reached roughly the halfway point, both hatches slammed shut and the bus shook with laughter. And there I remained for the next twenty minutes, shoeless, trying to look as nonchalant as possible while nearby passengers in cars and buses parked on the dock pointed fingers and giggled.

By the time we arrived in Dublin it was dark. There was an England match on telly and we had arranged to meet some of the Manchester crowd in a bar not far from the dock. The game was shite but by this time everyone was too drunk to care.

On arrival backstage at Slane the coach was parked about 75 metres from the back of the stage to ensure Shaun had a good chance of getting there on time. I took a walk into the field in front of the stage. The grass was wet and the sound of engines running generators filled the night with mechanical clatter. The stage was still being rigged by the lighting crew and every now and then a huge spot would sweep across the empty field. Tomorrow it would be filled with screaming crowds, stumbling casualties, hawkers, security and massive queues for bogs and beer. One of the crew arrived on a quad-bike and drove me to the back of the field which ran up a hill overlooking the stage and the castle. The field was surrounded by trees and edged with mobile food shops. The beer tent was at the crest of the hill to stage right and sixteen sets of barriers formed eight queues to the tent.

I sat down and lit a cigarette and watched the smoke curl up from my fingers. It was a still night and as the smoke rose it changed colour with the stage lights. I watched it do a circuit of red, blue, green, pink and then lay back and looked up at the stars. It was a fantastically clear night, the moon was fat and swollen and winking back down at the earth. The stars were hot-rock burns in the black duvet cover of the night. The chug of the generators had become no more than a background buzz and below me people were feverishly preparing, checking and double-checking that they could count on the equipment. Around the edge of the field the vendors were checking their buns, cold bags and cookers, and back at the bus the band were checking how much booze was left, and talking about heading off to a pub. It was about 10.30 p.m., but the nearest ale house was miles away so everyone settled in with a spliff and a Stella. Tomorrow was going to be a very busy day.

Slane Castle stands atop a commanding bank of the River Boyne about a mile west of the crossroads at Slane Village. The giant gothic stone castle gates are one of the first things you see of Slane village if you come in from Dublin. The whole area is steeped in history and there are said to be ancient Irish warriors buried in catacombs under the hill.

The castle itself was built by the Norman conquerors. The current nobility in residence is one Henry Lord Mountcharles, who pays for the upkeep of the place by allowing concerts on the castle lawn. Unfortunately the castle itself was gutted by fire in late 1991, shortly after U2 had been there to record their fourth album, *The Unforgettable Fire*. (I'm sure the irony wasn't lost on them.) The boarded-up windows remain and the whole process of restoration is still going on.

At 9 a.m. the whole bus was woken by the clatter of vehicles rolling into the backstage area. I say the whole bus, but there was no sign of Shaun for another three hours. Stepping out into the light the place looked a lot different than it did the night before. For a start we had managed to park right in front of three chemical toilets.

The St John's Ambulance people were holding a briefing in a tent right at the side of the stage, so I took a walk with Neil to find the dressing rooms. The Mondays' dressing room was a large portakabin with sofas, chairs, towels, shitloads of beer, wine, whisky and brandy and, most importantly, Paul Ryder's favourite – Yates's Australian White Wine with a kettle for making 'Blobs'.

The famous Blobs consist of Yates's white wine and a gloopy juice from down under, which you mix with hot water, lemon and sugar in a sort of hot-toddy style way, and it's gorgeous. At every gig Paul would bagsy the Yates's and if there wasn't any, Neil would have to send a runner out to get some from an off-licence or to buy a bottle by the measure from a pub. Rowetta was even worse. As soon as she arrived in the dressing room she would grab the Bushmills whisky and put it in her bag before anyone got their hands on it and the only person she would share it with was Shaun. I'm not saying she was a lush, she wasn't. She just didn't want anyone else getting their paws on her booze. And if they did, she'd make sure they knew about it.

Rowetta takes no shit, and she hates women. That's one of the reasons the Mondays have never really had any groupies – she scares them all off. She thinks girls are sly. She has one female friend and the rest are blokes and if any girls come near the band she will give them the sort of hard stare that would stop Paddington Bear in his tracks. And if that fails she'll probably just gob them.

Robbie Williams' dressing room, incidentally, was the mutt's nuts. He had a big conservatory-type affair with plush sofas and a big bowl of M&Ms on the table. There were curtains and even an extension and a private toilet so Robbie could safely stay inside if he wanted to.

Time moved on backstage and Neil was getting a bit unnerved because there was no sign of Wags or Paul who were supposed to be flying in that morning. People began to pile into the arena; it was like a floodgate opening as thousands of punters legged it for pole position by the stage. One by one all the bands arrived, but still no sign of the two missing Mondays.

Neil began making frantic phone calls, but couldn't get through to either Paul or Wags who had not turned up to meet their driver at the airport. When contacted, the driver said he hadn't seen them at all, and all sorts of horrific images started flashing through Neil's mind. Images of Wags still shopping in duty-free. Images of Paul getting to the airport and realising he'd forgotten his passport again. Then there was the possibility they could both still be in bed.

As Neil was flapping, his phone suddenly rang.

'Hello?' he said.

'Hello, this is Customs Officer Patrick O'Leary at Dublin Airport. Is that Mr Neil Mather?'

'Yes, it is. What can I do for you?' asked Neil, his heart sinking.

'Mr Mather, I have a Mr Paul Ryder and a Paul Wagstaff in custody here. They were stopped and searched after arriving on a flight from Manchester, England and were found to be carrying what we suspect are narcotic goods. They claim to be musicians and have asked me to contact you.'

'What are they being held for?'

'On suspicion of smuggling narcotics, Mr Mather.'

'Right. What's your address and telephone number?' said Neil, flapping more and more now.

'I need you to come down to the station straight away, Mr Mather.'

'Yeah, OK. What's your address?'

'I must stress, I need you to come down *straight away* sir.'

'Look, what's your phone number?' wailed Neil, sounding close to tears.

'Right, hold on a second, Mr Mather . . . *(what's the code for Dublin?)* er, Mr Mather, it's Dublin 7468976.'

At that Neil ran off to the site office to check the number, emerging a minute later visibly relieved to have discovered he was being wound up.

Oscar Wilde once said, 'Revenge is a dish best served cold,' and in my eyes it had long been time for an icy payback . . .

Weeks before, I had been asked by Neil to collect a certain parcel for an artist. Just as a favour, because he was busy with something else. I did so, and delivered it with the utmost speed and dexterity. But when the package was opened in front of the artist and about six other people it was empty. Neil then accused me of appropriating said goods in transit, while not only knowing full well that this wasn't the case but, as it later materialised, having had an orchestrating part in what was clearly seen at the time as the gag of the century.

So you can see that, despite risking the fury of Neil, getting my revenge was worth it. Just for those few moments of panic. For those few moments of imagining he'd have to tell the Slane Castle promoters that the gig was off. Of course, he'll probably deny he fell for it. But remember you heard it here first.

Wags and Paul did arrive eventually. They were caught in the traffic and in the end police outriders had to be found to escort them in. Ben Leach arrived in his old MG convertible about midday and announced he was engaged to his girlfriend Laura. *OK!* magazine wanted to park their new Bentley next to the Mondays bus so they could get pics of various people posing with it; of course they didn't *know* it was the Mondays bus, even though it was teeming with inebriated Mancunians. When they did finally realise whose bus it was, a big burly security guard was put on sentry duty to look after the Bentley.

Brian Molko and the Placebo gang were in the trailer next to us and because it was a sunny day everyone had brought their chairs outside and were sitting around chatting. After being passed a spliff by someone or other in one of the dressing rooms I went for a bleary-eyed walk and tried to give one of the brass section from Robbie Williams' band a blowback down his trumpet as he ran through his scales. Of course he politely declined for fear of oiling up his valves too much.

* * *

It was about 5 p.m. when the Mondays finally got their call to hit the stage. There was an air of finality in the music this time. Nothing morbid or sombre, but everyone seemed aware that this might be the end. At one point Shaun even did a little dance. If you blinked, you would have missed it, but it was definitely there. Just for a split second during 'Kinky Afro', he grooved to the music and shook his arms. Of course he denied it later. Like he always does.

During the final number, 'WFL', Nuts and Rowetta left the stage to taunt the front row of the crowd, following which Rowetta, brandishing her fearsome cat-o'-nine-tails, switched some poor security guard's arse within an inch of bleeding.

The set lasted about 60 minutes and then it was back to the dressing room and the bus for a big party. Everyone was going for it now. Paul Ryder had some genuine snuff which he was handing around, only to piss himself laughing as everyone nearly started sneezing uncontrollably after taking a hit. Then Robbie and his entourage arrived in Bentleys with a police escort and things really shifted a gear backstage.

Much credit to Robbie; he didn't play the pop star and go and hide in his super-posh changing room. He hung about and had a chat with everyone, especially Shaun and Paul. It must be good to meet people from way back, people who are down to earth and don't just tell you what you want to hear, which is what most people in the business seem to do.

Robbie was going to give us an interview for this book. When he found out me and Shaun were putting it together he came right over to where I was sitting with Paul Ryder and said, 'I'll give you a chat for your book, I've got some right stories to tell you!' Then he introduced me to his publicity agent, Gabby. 'I want to speak to this guy, Gabby,' he said. 'Get in touch with Gabby and we'll sort out a chat, I promise,' he told me.

Well, thanks Robbie but, PRs being what they are, every time I've called Gabby she's said you're far too busy. That's showbiz, I guess.

The rest of the day went by in a bit of a blur. Simon Moran and his colleague Mike Greek arrived, and there was some talk about what might happen in the future for the band. It was decided that there should be a meeting some time over the next few weeks to decide where to go next for the Mondays.

Before we left, I went up to the side of the stage with Wags's mam and daughter to watch Robbie Williams begin his set. As the opening bars of 'Let Me Entertain You' rang out, it was as though all his muscles went loose and he began doing some kind of bizarre, loose-limbed contortion act. For a second I couldn't place it, but then I realised. Robbie must have stolen it from Bez!

Suddenly he stiffened and ran on stage in time to deliver his opening line. But as he sang and the crowd exploded into chorus with him I was left with just this vivid vision of his freaky octopus-like warm-up technique. Must be a rock'n'roll thing.

BEN LEACH: I really enjoyed the tour. The best thing that happened about the whole Mondays thing was I met my girlfriend Laura. Paul set us up on a blind date; he'd known Laura and a friend of hers, who's now his partner, for years. He had been down in London and Laura asked him if he had any mates – she was looking for a boyfriend or something. And he said, 'Yeah, I do actually.' So I spoke to her on the phone a few times, went down to London and met her in an Indian restaurant. We're getting married in May 2000.

The bus was ready to rumble and Neil had warned everyone on pain of death to be there on time or it would be leaving without them.

And for once everyone *was* there on time. Robbie was just starting his fourth song when the gates opened, and we roared away into the night. Of course Neil had arranged with security to clear the road so we would have a clear passage out on to the main road out of Slane and towards Dublin. Which is why after 50 yards we ground to a halt and spent the next hour and a half in heavy traffic trying to get out of the grounds.

As we sat in the bus, leaving the screaming crowds behind us, contemplating the traffic jam ahead, it brought home to me the adage which sums up their spectacular, hilarious reunion tour. The tour that happened after most of the band had decided to quit the music business. The tour that Bez had turned down flat because he didn't want to be part of another heroin-fuelled cabaret show. The tour that included a man called Nuts who had gone on holiday in Ibiza and ending up meeting Shaun Ryder and becoming the new Monday. The tour that miraculously came together despite Paul's vow never to speak to his brother again.

The adage? *Whatever happens is whatever happens.*

6. RYDER 'GOD-LIKE GENIUS' – OFFICIAL

X and Row deny lovechild, Bez wipes out dry stone wall, Shaun mistakes eggy liqueur for barrister, gives Chris Moyles tongue, Shaun and Bez see off Eric Clapton, Bez thanks the Lord, band fail to have meeting.

All in all the Mondays tour was a runaway success. The weeks of solid practice had paid off and in total they played eighteen dates around the world to rave reviews . . . but what now?

It was mooted that over the weeks following the tour there would be a meeting to discuss the future of the band and the possibility of recording a new album. There was also talk that SJM wanted them to play another couple of gigs around Christmas time.

The meeting, of course, never happened.

Over the next few months the band drifted apart again. Paul Ryder moved to London to be with his girlfriend Angie. At one point the showbiz columns were filled with rumours of Shaun and Rowetta living together and having a baby. But the rumours were untrue and had been leaked by a member of the crew who overheard and misinterpreted a joking conversation between the pair.

Shaun didn't buy anywhere to live, so a pal converted the cellar of his house into a luxury studio apartment for him complete with TV, video, stereo and PlayStation. For a while he considered investing in a pub in Gorton, but never got around to it.

Nuts, meanwhile, had been roped in to help his girlfriend re-decorate her new house, and Ben finally managed to move out of Neil's place and escape back down to London where he moved in with Laura.

Wags began hitting the DJ circuit, living in Manchester and playing at local clubs like 42nd Street and the Rock'n'Roll Bar, as well as a few London venues. Lee Mullen went back to working Saturday nights at The Ritz and giving drum lessons, before moving down to London to work on a West End show. And Gaz Whelan carried on being Gaz.

And then of course there was Bez, the man you couldn't make up. The man who is at once the luckiest and the unluckiest person alive. Bez, who has had more near-death experiences with cars, jeeps, drugs and illness than the sum total of all the people Arthur C. Clarke has ever met in his mysterious world. If Bez was unlucky enough to fall out of a plane he would land in a vat of feathers in a pillow factory AND find a tenner in there.

Well, Bez took over writing a motorbike column in *Front* magazine on top of his usual 'Bez Sez' page. It was unpaid but gave him the chance to meet his biking heroes and ride some incredible machines. The role also secured him lifetime free insurance from one company who wanted to use him for their advertising pictured beside a machine with the caption: *'We'll Even Insure Bez!'*

It was while testing out a new bike in the Scottish lowlands that Bez came a cropper. The true story is still shaded in some mystery and embarrassment, but according to Shaun, Bez was being given riding lessons from World Superbike champion Carl Fogarty. It seems Bez failed to heed the racer's words when warned not to try and keep up with Fogarty who was going for a 'burn'. But Bez thought, Piece of piss, pulled back on the throttle and wiped out on a bend, flying straight into a stone wall.

Bez broke a collarbone and two ribs. He was taken to a Scottish hospital where he developed a dangerous blood infection and came within a hair's breadth of popping his clogs. Thankfully, the medics managed to save him. He stayed in hospital for Christmas and New Year, receiving regular visits from the other Mondays who would take him on a 'burn' round the hospital in a wheelchair, and was finally transferred to a Manchester hospital in January. He went home in February 2000.

Shaun, meanwhile, seems to be in his most serious relationship for a long time, with a girl he met on a night out in Manchester. She works in theatre and they have moved in together. These days he rarely goes out, preferring to stay in with a spliff and a whisky, watching the telly rather than having it massive in town. He's not exactly Mr Pipe And Slippers, but his priorities have changed since the old days. He doesn't need to go out and be seen any more, preferring the quiet anonymity of a life baked in the warming glow of his TV to being recognised in the street. These days he even does the washing up.

Musically, though, he has stayed busy since the last Mondays gig. A version of Donovan's 'Barabajagal' had been recorded during the final practice week in Birmingham, with the Dope Smugglaz and Howard Marks, and the release date was now set for May 2000. And in a twist even more bizarre than Ian Brown recording Michael Jackson songs, Shaun put together an incredible version of 'Barcelona' with an opera singer pal who is hoping to release it as a single.

In February 2000 Shaun was invited to the *NME* Awards Ceremony to receive a Lifetime Achievement Award for Godlike Genius. He shared the front cover of the mag with Sir Paul McCartney, who picked up the gong for 'Best Band In The World'. Shaun's *Sport* column the following week described the event:

GOD-LIKE GENIUS

ALRIGHT dudes, it's Shaun Ryder and now I am officially a god-like genius because the *NME* have said so. Not that we all didn't know that anyway.

The award itself is brilliant – it's a fist giving the one-fingered salute. It will look great next to the other one . . . in the pawn shop.

But I'll tell you one thing. I've just got back from the ceremony in London and I am hungover to f***, man.

Everyone was there: Sir Paul McCartney, the Royle Family, Blur, Keith Allen and a load of indie bands that I've never f***ing ever heard of and who all seemed to be Welsh.

And I must say Damon Albarn from Blur is putting on weight since becoming a dad, he's a bit more sausage roll than rock'n'roll these days.

Steve Lamacq and the gorgeous Mary Anne Hobbs did the presenting for most of the show, but I got mine off Steve Sutherland, the boss of *NME*, and I must admit I was a bit choked up but I don't think anyone noticed.

And then me and Macca posed for some pics before heading off to the party. Which is where it all starts to get a bit foggy really.

The party was at the Mermaid Theatre in London, and there was a fantastic view across the Thames, I remember that much.

But there wasn't enough free booze which is a shame. The bash is sponsored by Carling Premier so that's all you got given to drink, anything else you had to pay for.

Oh, and there were a couple of bottles of bubbly on everyone's table along with some wine, but that all lasted about 34 seconds once we got there.

I met up with the old Mondays manager Nathan McGough, who's looking after a band called Shack. It was good to bury the hatchet because we didn't part on the best of terms six years ago.

And then I seem to remember some bloke called Howard who wouldn't let anyone get a word in edgeways turned up with a bottle of vodka from somewhere, climbed on a windowsill, started shouting and sent a table crashing over; which is when I thought it would be a good time to f*** off before someone decided to blame me for it, which is what usually happens.

There were a few punch-ups I heard, but nothing spectacular. Some bloke from *TFI Friday* was whizzing about flicking everyone on the ear with an elastic band though.

Anyway then we f***ed off to the Met Bar for some ridiculously overpriced drinks at about 3 a.m. before finally heading off to the hotel to check in, only to find out that a room had been reserved for my mate Warbs but not for me! Bastard.

F*** knows what time it was by now but we phoned Steve Sutherland to sort it all out, and finally got another room sorted on a different floor.

> Woke up about 3 p.m. the next day, felt like absolute shite, and Adidas sent me a big bag of goodies to bring home on the train including a top jacket and a pair of trainers.
>
> Watch *TFI Friday* this week if you get the chance and you'll see the geezer who went around flicking people's ears with the laccy band, I think he got Fatboy Slim and Boy George too.

The Mondays' notoriety has now reached epic proportions. Legends abound about the freakshow-cum-slapstick-comedy that is the band and their entourage. Nearly everyone in showbusiness has now either run into them or run away from them. And whilst clinging for dear life to the shirt-tails of their mad, messy reunion tour, I collected a few gems:

TONY WILSON: *NME* wanted an interview with Shaun and Carl Denver in the Channel Islands. Fine, we had *Top Of The Pops* to do on Wednesday, so we thought Shaun and Nathan would fly to Jersey with the *NME* journalists to see Carl Denver who was doing cabaret there.

They went to London, they got the journalists, they got on the plane and suddenly I got a phone call from Nathan. I said, 'Naths, what is it?' And he said, 'It's fucking Shaun – they stopped him at customs, with an empty plastic bag on him and there's traces of something in it. As soon as we got there they fucking arrested him.'

It was about four in the afternoon. We'd got a lawyer lined up, we were in court the next morning, but the message came back that Shaun wouldn't talk to anyone, not even an advocate. We sent the rest of the band down to Shepherd's Bush to be ready for *Top Of The Pops* but we couldn't get anyone in to see him. He wouldn't talk to us.

At about 10.20 the next morning I got a call from Nathan: 'Tell the BBC we got bail and we're on our way. OK, bye!' As the plane was flying over the Channel, Nathan turned to Shaun and said: 'Why wouldn't you see a lawyer? Why wouldn't you talk to anyone?'

'What do you mean? I always want to see my brief, I was wondering where you were. What you talking about, that's a pile of shite!' said Shaun. 'Tell you what, though. Fucking weird them pigs in Jersey, man, fucking weird.'

'What do you mean?' Nathan said.

Shaun replied, 'Well, they kept offering me a drink. They kept opening the cell door and saying do you want an Advocaat. So I kept saying, "Fuck off!"'

CHRIS MOYLES: I met Shaun once when we were doing a roadshow in Wales. He goes [best Manc accent] 'Alright man how are you?' I'd never met the man before in my life. He said ' 'Ere you are, mate, I've got a present for you,' and handed a packet to me. I opened it cautiously, only to find it was a packet of tongue.

Why had he brought me tongue? Well, I'd bitten my tongue a month before that in Scotland, and I had to go to casualty in Glasgow, and I'd been bitching about it on my radio show. So it turned out Shaun was a big fan of the show and he'd come down to see the roadshow, so we pissed off to the pub across the road.

I introduced him to my mum and my dad and my brother and my auntie, and he sat talking to my mum for about an hour, and he never swore once and was the nicest man you could ever meet in your life. And from this day on, if you ever say 'Shaun Ryder' to my mother, she'll say, 'Oh he's lovely, how is he, such a nice young man.' There he was talking to my old mum about Ireland, and she's telling him to go and get a haircut.

CHARLES BRONSON (Britain's Most Violent Prisoner): I admire Shaun Ryder for his lifestyle and his manliness, in the sense that no one is ever going to tell him what to do. He's a real rebel, and he walks his own path. I have maximum respect for the man.

NIGEL PIVARO: I first met Shaun at Ambrose Barlow, the secondary modern school. He was in the first year when I was in the third year. Now, he claims I was the main perpetrator of his initiation into Ambrose Barlow, you know the usual thing, getting a bit roughed up and stuff.

He looked like he had a bit of an edge to him even then, but he didn't yet have the physical weight to back it up. He was one of those that every now and then I'd slap around a bit to remind him not to get above his station.

CLINT BOON (Inspiral Carpets): He was a dude, a proper dude, Shaun, despite how he used to slag us off in the press. On the new album, the first track is called 'Presley on Oldham Street' and it refers to that whole Madchester period, and particularly to seeing Shaun walking down Oldham Street and me thinking 'He's the modern Presley!' That's how highly I thought of him as an artist, as a Presley for Manchester.

I always looked up to the Mondays, I always thought they were a dead smart band and I was always in awe of them to a large extent. The Inspirals – we had all these good songs, and we were pretty clean-cut and industrious and all that. But the Mondays just had something so totally spontaneous and organic about them; every time I came away from a Mondays gig I would be thinking, I'm going to pack it in, because I always felt they were just so much better than what I was doing. But then a couple of days after I would be like, No fuck it, we'll keep on doing what we're doing.

In August 1999, music Magazine *Q* published a list of the Top 100 Greatest Stars of the 20th Century, as voted for by their readers. It was topped by John Lennon, with Sir Paul McCartney in second. Elvis Presley, Kurt Cobain and Bob Dylan made up the rest of the Top Five.

Shaun Ryder and Mark Berry ranked at 68 and 78 respectively. Not bad for a pair of reformed hard drug users and petty criminals, to find themselves voted as being more important than the likes of Elvis Costello,

Eric Clapton and half of Pink Floyd – Waters and Barrett to be precise. Shaun was sandwiched between Prince (The Artist Formerly Known As 'Good') and dub pioneer Lee Scratch Perry. The magazine described him thus: *'If drug taking were the sole qualification for rock stardom, then Shaun Ryder would gain instant access to our hall of fame . . . and probably burgle it.'*

Bez, the man who can't sing, write music or play an instrument was well chuffed to be included ahead of Damon Albarn and Sting. In fact he was sandwiched between Led Zep's Robert Plant and the mistress of Motown Diana Ross. The very fact that Bez was included on the list is incredible. But the fact that he is the only person in the entire 100 who has never written a song or learned to play an instrument is awesome.

Q's target readership are the twenty- to thirty-somethings who grew up with the Mondays. The potheads turned professionals who have swapped spliffs for sauvignon blanc. Who have hung up their baggy denim and long-sleeved tops in exchange for the *de rigeur* combat pants of graphic designers, and the suits of salesmen and accountants. These are the people who voted for the mad pair. And what a mad pair they were.

Shaun needed Bez like Bez needed Shaun. One, the lyricist whose words enraptured a generation of pilled-up acid house party people; the other a manic, staring, off-his-trolley freaky dancer whose bulging eyes and foaming mouth embodied the message, spirit and character of the band and the times. For a short while Bez *was* the Zeitgeist. He was the spirit of the age. He is still the visual cue who gives flashbacks to a generation. Flashbacks to the time Ecstasy arrived in Britain and people spent years getting off their nuts at the end of the eighties and beginning of the nineties.

In terms of a partnership, Shaun and Bez have no precedent; they go together more like hippies and Glastonbury than Lennon and McCartney.

> **TONY WILSON:** There isn't a comparison for them in rock'n'roll. It's not a Jagger and Richards thing, because Jagger sings and Richards plays guitar. The lead singer and the lead dancer are a very odd couple.
>
> For most people their biggest value is not the value of the songwriting or the value of the performer, their biggest value is the value as cultural icons. Icons are central to pop culture in general and pop music in particular, and Bez was iconic. Because of his look, because of his attitude, because he played the part of a pop star. Ringo Starr was a major character in the 60s, and he said to John Lennon once during recording: 'John, stop shouting at me, I'm not the best drummer in the world!' to which John Lennon replied: 'Listen, sunshine, you're not the best fucking drummer in the Beatles.' I would put Ringo's musical contribution as about on the same par as Bez's. But Ringo had a look, an aura. I think the nearest thing you can get to the concept of Bez was Ringo Starr. And Ringo was important. Being a terrible musician is pretty fucking irrelevant. Technical proficiency in musicians is the death of rock'n'roll. They should become musicians by accident.

Shaun, Gaz and Paul all think they've got another album left in them. The difficult thing is getting them all back together. Early on in 2000 Paul moved back to Manchester with his then pregnant girlfriend Angie, who has set up a film company in the same building Factory Records once occupied. Paul has since teamed up with Gaz and Lee Mullen on a musical project called Buffalo 66. The name is correct at the time of going to press, but is currently being changed more often than a woman's mind.

Rowetta somehow landed a job as casting director for the film *Social Soup*, which is due to begin shooting in January 2000. She's also working on a dance track with Paul Davis.

Bez is convalescing, counting his lucky stars after his high-speed meeting with a wall, and looking to the future:

BEZ: I've had a lot of top experiences and I thank the Lord and pray they'll all keep coming because I get really bored when it's quiet. I'm not religious, I don't know what I am, but I'm always grateful to whoever's in charge of the big picture, you know what I mean. I don't know if I've had my best time, I think the best is always to come.

I have my home where I live with my family. I've spread my seed, my genes, so I have to take responsibility some time. I want to bring my kids up in comfort so they don't have to think about going robbing or anything like that, so I've got to earn some dough. I can see Shaun doing the same. X can do anything he wants, if he doesn't do smack and crack.

I say there's fuck-all wrong with doing drugs, but there's doing drugs in an alright way and there's doing drugs in a bad way. I wouldn't recommend anyone to do them but basically I enjoy it, I like smoking my weed because it makes me chill and I can listen to my tunes and really get into it. That's the way for me and I like to take an E when I go out because I like to be sociable and I like to dance. I like the way it makes the music sound phenomenal. But I don't drink that much. I'd rather spend my last £5 on weed than on a couple of pints of beer.

For the future it's motorbikes, writing, music, Mondays, snowboarding, just having a good time, bringing up my kids the best I can, giving them the best time I can along the way and generally being as nice as I can to everyone I meet and spreading good feelings.

In the same month that Bez went home from hospital after his biking accident, the Mondays were asked to play support for Oasis during the UK leg of the band's world tour. It's unlikely the Ryder brothers will ever bury the hatchet, but for the time being it looks like they're still prepared to play together, despite their unfathomable differences. The brothers' relationship is steeped in more history than Rome itself. And Shaun's still not speaking to his dad.

For now though, the taxman is off his back, and more importantly Shaun's remembering how to enjoy life again. In March 2000, when the *Melody Maker* held a poll of the biggest hellraisers in the music business ever, Shaun Ryder came second. Not only did he come second, he was the only living person in the top three. Sandwiched between Keith Moon in third and Kurt Cobain in first place sat Shaun Ryder. More than anything this shows that Shaun and the Mondays will be remembered as much for their antics as their music. For the culture of excess they endorsed. It could also mean that he's lucky to be alive after years of rock'n'roll excess, or that he's a harder party animal than the rest. But for Shaun William Ryder, as for Bez, the drugs were there before the business. Cobain and Moon were from different backgrounds, real contenders for rock'n'roll suicide; for them, drugs were the new thing. For Shaun the *music* was the new thing; the drugs were always there, and always will be.

As for what the future holds for Happy Mondays, we can only guess at the moment. They still haven't had that meeting, though.

SHAUN: All in all, the tour was a real success. It ended up being a real pleasure working with Bez and Gaz and the Mondays again. Wags is a great musician who worked with me in Black Grape, and he's a very good writer. And Ben is a good writer as well.

We probably will do another album. If we do another album we'll do more shows. But it's got to be a proper album and it's got to be done the way I want it done. The only thing that's stopped us so far is Paul. For six years my brother was having a breakdown, never did anything. Then the Mondays got back together and within a couple of months our Paul's in competition with me because I had a Number One album and a Number Seven album with Black Grape. He's got this thing about trying to prove himself, as though he didn't spend six years on his arse.

We could have made something good, but people are finding Paul hard to work with now. Oh and at one point our kid is saying he owns the name 'Happy Mondays'. What's he going to do? Go out as 'Paul Ryder's Happy Mondays' and get a fake Bez in and do all the working men's clubs? After six years, you think he'd have learned a lesson of how to be a bit more realistic, how to view the business. But he hasn't, he's jumped back into it and after a few months back together with the Mondays he's making the exact same mistakes as he did last time.

For the Mondays it's a shame because Gaz is a great drummer and a great musician, Wags is great and I've still got things we could do. The reason the last Mondays album wasn't successful was because I didn't have any part in it. I was always more of a director, saying can we try this, or can we try that. I always treated it as a firm. But once the firm breaks up and people start believing they're more important than the others, that's when it falls apart.

I've got some ideas and I'm going to do some of my own stuff. I'll be going into the studio at the end of 2000. If we do it as the Happy Mondays, then great. I'd like to work with Bez, I'd like to work with Gaz, and Wags. If not I'll be working with Wags to make a record and I'll bring it out under my own name. After this next tour with Oasis it might be the end of the Mondays, we can't just carry on playing the old material. But whatever happens it's not the end of me, I've been in the music business for so long. From the Mondays I went straight into Black Grape. I've never not been doing any music, I've never stopped. But before the Mondays got back together I'd had a break and I needed that to fucking get my sanity back after spending the eighties and the nineties on the road. I had a break from it and I got my zest back and I'm ready to make some more music.

Along the mad and twisted way the Mondays have made plenty of friends and plenty of enemies. Most would say their biggest enemies are themselves and the drugs. The drugs which became their selling point, their appeal and finally their undoing. A poison and a panacea, a prescription for both life and death, each a cure for the other in equal measures. Shaun Ryder, one of the twentieth century's greatest contenders for rock'n'roll suicide has continuously confounded his greatest critics simply by staying alive. And Bez . . . well . . . you know what I mean!?

The Mondays are important, there's no denying that. Important for the way they took the sterile animal that was the pop world and not so much turned it on its head as ran up behind it with a broken bottle and took its dinner money. It was the Happy Mondays who struck fear into the hearts of their contemporaries with their backstage boozing, brawling and excessive drug-taking; it was the Happy Mondays who gave every mother in the land a clear idea of the sort of person she *didn't* want her daughter coming home with at night;

and it was the Happy Mondays who made the tunes that changed the face of partying. That is their legacy, their little slice of immortality. But is that it?

The Mondays' legend will always live on outside of the music: not least through the stories, which have become folklore in the music business. They have touched the lives of many people, from the fans to the record companies, and changed them all a little bit; whether by showing how life can be lived as a non-stop party or just by showing people it's a bad idea to lend a motor vehicle to a man with more drugs in his veins than in the whole of ICI. Everyone has a story to tell about the Mondays. And mine was about seeing Shaun Ryder going from a seemingly down-and-out junkie existence in an unfurnished room in Burnley to once more taking his place as one of Britain's most celebrated musicians.

STEVE LAMACQ: I think there are enough stories about the Happy Mondays for people to keep talking about them for years on end, to be honest. Bands live on through myth, really, myth and legends. There are so many people who grew up with the Mondays, or who enjoyed being part of the circle round them, that they're gonna be telling these stories for years and years even if the Mondays pack up and you never hear of Shaun Ryder again. There'll still be people saying, 'I remember the days . . .' and, 'Let me tell you about the Hacienda, young man.'

I think the Mondays' myth grows; they disappear for a bit, and the myth just grows again. And every time they disappear people go, 'Oh, the

Mondays, there'll never ever be anything like the Mondays.'

SHAUN: Do I think the Mondays will go down in musical history? I couldn't give a fuck.

INDEX